PRAISE FOR *Catholic Wisdo*

D0729197

From the moment I opened *Catholic Wisdom* ... ... moment I closed it, I felt as if I had been bathed in an abundance of graces which lifted up my heart and soul. Donna's recipes are delectable and power-packed! Each chapter consists of various combinations of the following: enlightening excerpts from papal encyclicals on love and the family, brief passages from the *Catechism of the Catholic Church* as well as the Holy Bible, penetrating quotes from some of my favorite saints (St. Thérèse of Lisieux, St. Maximilian Kolbe, St. Augustine, St. John of the Cross, and many more), personal anecdotes, practical tips, and so much more. This was truly a work of love that will lift up mothers in their vocations, help them see what their true role is according to God's will, and encourage them in the challenging role that they face in society today.

—JEAN M. HEIMANN, catholicfire.blogspot.com

"Donna has given us the beautiful gift of 'recipes' we can follow to bring peace, joy, and happiness into our day—helping us to create the kind of home that makes holy families!"

—SALLY ROBB, wife, mother of six,
and host on Catholic Radio International

Whether you're a fan of books about motherhood or not (I'm usually not), you'll find this conversation with Donna-Marie Cooper O'Boyle to be just the thing to encourage you in your vocation as a mother. It's a boost of support, and not just for Catholics! All Christian mothers will benefit from Cooper O'Boyle's wisdom and advice, and will find themselves discovering the satisfaction of their vocation.

—SARAH REINHARD, snoringscholar.com

OTHER BOOKS
BY DONNA-MARIE COOPER O'BOYLE

Donna-Marie is the author of more than twenty-five books,
including these that are referenced in this book.

The Domestic Church: Room by Room

Embracing Motherhood

Feeding Your Family's Soul

Mother Teresa and Me: Ten Years of Friendship

The Kiss of Jesus: How Mother Teresa and the Saints Helped Me to
Discover the Beauty of the Cross

for CATHOLIC WISDOM
A MOTHER'S HEART

DONNA-MARIE COOPER O'BOYLE

PARACLETE PRESS
BREWSTER, MASSACHUSETTS

2018 First Printing

Catholic Wisdom for a Mother's Heart

Copyright © 2018 by Donna-Marie Cooper O'Boyle

ISBN 978-1-61261-922-4

Library of Congress Cataloging-in-Publication Data
Names: O'Boyle, Donna-Marie Cooper, author.
Title: Catholic wisdom for a mother's heart / Donna-Marie Cooper O'Boyle.
Description: Brewster, MA : Paraclete Press, Inc., 2018. | Includes
    bibliographical references.
Identifiers: LCCN 2018001883 | ISBN 9781612619224 (trade paper)
Subjects: LCSH: Mothers—Religious life. | Catholic women—Religious life. |
    Motherhood—Religious aspects—Catholic Church. | Parenting—Religious
    aspects—Catholic Church. | Child rearing—Religious aspects—Catholic Church.
Classification: LCC BX2353 .O24 2018 | DDC 248.8/431088282—dc23
LC record available at https://lccn.loc.gov/2018001883

10 9 8 7 6 5 4 3 2 1

Published by Paraclete Press
Brewster, Massachusetts
www.paracletepress.com
Printed in the United States of America

With all of my heart to all of my children:
Justin, Chaldea, Jessica, Joseph, and Mary-Catherine.
And to my grandchildren:
Shepherd James and Leo Arthur.
May God continually bless you all
with his grace and love!

The Church gives thanks for all the manifestations of the feminine "genius" which have appeared in the course of history, in the midst of all peoples and nations; she gives thanks for all the charisms which the Holy Spirit distributes to women in the history of the People of God, for all the victories which she owes to their faith, hope and charity: she gives thanks for all the fruits of feminine holiness.

The Church asks at the same time that these invaluable "manifestations of the Spirit" (cf. 1 Cor 12:4ff), which with great generosity are poured forth upon the "daughters" of the eternal Jerusalem, may be attentively recognized and appreciated so that they may return for the common good of the Church and of humanity, especially in our times. Meditating on the biblical mystery of the "woman," the Church prays that in this mystery all women may discover themselves and their "supreme vocation."

—Mulieris Dignitatem, 31

CONTENTS

I grew up loving and being loved by the world's best mother. The sad truth is that I didn't truly appreciate the many gifts my mother had bestowed upon me until I accepted and embraced my own vocation to motherhood. Somehow, when my son Eric was born, my eyes were opened to the sacrifices my mother had made on my behalf. But even more importantly, I came to full realization of the most prized treasure she had shared with my siblings and me—a true love for my faith and a personal relationship with a God who loves me unconditionally.

Having known my dear friend Donna-Marie Cooper O'Boyle for many years now, I have often noted the similarities between her and my own mother. Like my mom, who raised five of us, Donna-Marie has always been fully committed to the physical, emotional, and spiritual formation of the three girls and two boys who are at the center of her universe. Now as a grandmother, Donna-Marie's compassion continues to extend to a beautiful new generation.

Although the physical distance that separates us has kept Donna-Marie and me from seeing each other in person often, I "know" my precious friend even more intimately through the gift of her writing. Through her books, columns, and blogs, Donna-Marie has helped me more frequently than she will ever know. Just like my own mother, Donna-Marie's witness to the mission of motherhood continues to inspire me to embrace my own path daily.

Catholic Wisdom for a Mother's Heart is the book I wish I'd had when my own sons—now both young adults—were toddlers. I spent too many years stressing out over things that don't really matter and missed a lot of opportunities along the way. The good news for me, and for you as well, is that our vocation to motherhood is a lifelong joy. The occasions to grow spiritually along with our children are as fresh and new each day as the morning dew glistening below each lovely sunrise.

Whether you are pregnant or awaiting the adoption of a child, foster-parenting, raising teens, or parenting adult children (as my mother still does every day for her five children and our spouses), the gift of motherhood continues to evolve in new and wonderful ways. The wisdom contained in *Catholic Wisdom for a Mother's Heart* is always relevant. Donna-Marie has done the difficult work of meticulously compiling a treasure trove of resources to guide and instruct us in the sublime responsibilities that accompany our role as mothers.

References to papal encyclicals, the *Catechism of the Catholic Church*, and Holy Scripture are organized and presented to us in a way that complements the "real-world" issues that Donna-Marie discusses in her book. Donna-Marie shares the wisdom of the saints, our daily role models for virtuous living. In addition, we as readers benefit from Donna-Marie's personal relationship and correspondence with two heroes of our faith, Father John A. Hardon, sj, and St. Teresa of Calcutta. The cumulative effect of Donna-Marie's work is a book that is at once impeccably researched and endearingly personal.

Each of us, in our own unique ways and with our own special set of circumstances, has been called specially by God to the vocation of motherhood. With *Catholic Wisdom for a Mother's Heart*, Donna-Marie Cooper O'Boyle reminds us that we are each uniquely equipped to respond to God's trust in us to raise up our families to know and to love Him unceasingly. In the heart of our homes, we have the capacity to change our own little corners of the world through the love, compassion, and spiritual gifts we shower upon our children. Strengthened with prayer, we moms and our families are on the spiritual journey of a lifetime, filled with sacrifices, occasional struggles, and moments of great joy.

As you enjoy the pearls of wisdom and caring that are served up in *Catholic Wisdom for a Mother's Heart*, I hope you will join me in praying for other mothers around the world as we each walk our own unique vocational paths. I also hope that you will consider sharing the gift of *Catholic Wisdom for a Mother's Heart* with a special person in your life who may also be strengthened and encouraged by Donna-Marie's apostolate of love.

I continually give thanks for my own mother, who lives out on a daily basis the precepts that Donna-Marie shares with us in *Catholic Wisdom for a Mother's Heart*. Like my mother,

Donna-Marie Cooper O'Boyle is the type of mom I can only hope to be someday—happy, holy, and beloved by children who are well on their way to lives that will make a difference in this world. I would like to personally thank Donna-Marie for the ongoing gift of her friendship and for acting as a constant source of inspiration and enlightenment.

—Lisa M. Hendey, founder of CatholicMom.com

Dear St. John Paul II said, "Motherhood is a woman's vocation. It is an eternal vocation, and it is also a contemporary vocation. . . . We must do everything in order that woman may merit love and veneration. We must do everything in order that children, the family and society may see in her that dignity that Christ saw." Motherhood today is not necessarily viewed as a noble or dignified vocation. Unfortunately, in many areas, society continues to value a person simply by the size of their paycheck, and therefore some mothers might not feel very confident in their role of raising their children. Our culture does not acknowledge the invaluable sacrifices and love in raising little saints to heaven. Add to that, today's mothers don't have many opportunities to receive a pat on the back for a job well done. Not that they are looking for any recognition, but a little affirmation here and there would be nice. Pope Francis pointed out, "Every human person owes his or her life to a mother, and almost always owes much of what follows in life, both human and spiritual formation, to her. Yet, despite being highly lauded from a symbolic point of view—many poems, many beautiful things said poetically of her—the mother is rarely listened to or helped in daily life, rarely considered central to society in her role."

The many mixed messages about women's rights and where a woman should find her place in society can make one dizzy! Additionally, our culture does not often encourage mothers to consider the role that prayer plays in a family's life or that motherhood is a sublime vocation. Moreover, family members may not always express their appreciation for the tireless work and care given from their mother, which may cause a mom to feel a bit neglected and unacknowledged. What's a Catholic mother to do?

First of all, let's keep our chins up and know in our hearts that we Catholic mothers need not feel alone and are—in reality—sisters in Christ on this journey together! We can certainly all benefit from encouragement and praise to aid and uplift us on our pilgrimage throughout the challenging vocation of motherhood. We can extend a hand to help each other along the way. How fortunate we are to have been blessed with leaders in our Church, such as St. John Paul II, Pope Benedict XVI, and Pope Francis, and those before them who have always extolled mothers with their wonderful words of praise, acknowledging a mother's sublime role. Pope Francis underscored a mother's selfless and irreplaceable role when he said, "Mothers are the strongest antidote to the spread of self-centered individualism. 'Individual' means 'what cannot be divided'. Mothers, instead, 'divide' themselves, from the moment they bear a child to give him to the world and help him grow."

We can all play an important role in our world today to be of assistance to other mothers we meet who are not quite aware of God's plan in their mothering, and we can help them to discover their God-given gifts and their high dignity in Our Lord's eyes.

Let us ponder St. John Paul II's words:

> It is a disservice not only to children but also to women and society itself when a woman is made to feel guilty for wanting to remain in the home and nurture and care for her children. It is also necessary to counter the misconception that the role of motherhood is oppressive to women and that a commitment to her family, particularly to her children, prevents a woman from reaching personal fulfillment and from having an influence in society. No response to women's issues can ignore a woman's role in the family or take lightly the fact that every new life is entrusted to the protection and care of the woman carrying it in the womb.

These are undoubtedly powerful and profound words to call to mind, especially if doubts arise within our own personal journeys and when attempting to help other mothers who have lost their way or are not sure what direction to pursue. Our example speaks volumes, and our kind words in response to women seeking direction in finding and achieving personal fulfillment can be very transforming, by God's grace.

Throughout my ministry to mothers, I have observed that Christian mothers everywhere are looking for strategies to help improve their prayer lives, their understanding of their Faith, and their role in their home life as well. Like-minded women are feeling a vital and even urgent need to communicate with one another, comparing notes to discover the best approaches to mothering with grace as is very apparent in the many Catholic mothers' blogs that have been popping up all over the Internet and the many mothers' groups that are gathering together in homes, parishes, or online to participate in studies about their Catholic faith. I have also found that even though we mothers are surrounded by many confusing messages targeting women, there is an encouraging authentic resurgence of Christian women who are fighting through it all, thirsting for the truth. This is very heartwarming. God's grace abounds! These women are tomorrow's saints.

Mothering my own five children for the past forty-plus years has given me deep happiness, wisdom from the "trenches," and also plenty of stories to tell! I humbly offer Catholic mothers "recipes" and advice for seeking and finding a deep and enriching spiritual life while remaining attentive to their families. My prayer is that this book will serve mothers well and that they will find encouragement, praise, camaraderie, and direction throughout its pages.

Dear mothers, enjoy reading, reflecting, and pondering on the material in this book. I hope it will be inspiring food for your soul and that you will *feel* your well-deserved pat on the back! Make yourself a steaming cup of tea or coffee, and sit and take a little time to refresh your soul. Allow this book to serve you, taking in nourishment from its flavorful recipes for faithful mothering. Be at peace so that you may guide your family well with joy and love within your amazing vocation—lighting your family's way to heaven!

Let's be confident, knowing that by loving our families, dedicating our vocations to the Lord, and seeking assistance from the Blessed Mother, as well as intercession from the saints, we will be "making our lives something beautiful for God," as my friend St. Teresa of Calcutta used to say.

St. John Paul II has assured us that "the dignity and responsibility of the Christian family as the domestic Church can be achieved only with God's unceasing aid, which will surely be granted if it is humbly and trustingly petitioned in prayer" (*Familiaris Consortio*, 59). Let's be sure to ask Our Lord for his unceasing aid. Let us sisters in Christ stick together, encourage one another, and continue our prayers for each other and our families within our domestic churches, as we mother our families with grace. May God bless us all!

The hour is coming, indeed has come, in which the vocation of women is being acknowledged in its fullness; the hour in which women acquire in the world an influence, an effect, and a power never hitherto achieved. That is why at this moment, when the human race is undergoing so deep a transformation, women, imbued with the spirit of the Gospel, can do so much to aid mankind in not falling.

—*From the Closing Documents of Vatican II*

MOTHER

The Most Important Person on earth is a mother.

She cannot claim the honor of having built Notre
   Dame Cathedral.

She need not.

She has built something more magnificent than any
   cathedral—

a dwelling for an immortal soul, the tiny perfection
   of her baby's body. . . .

The angels have not been blessed with such a
   grace.

They cannot share in God's creative miracle to
   bring new saints to Heaven.

Only a human mother can.

Mothers are closer to God the Creator than any
   other creature;

God joins forces with mothers in performing this
   act of creation. . . .

What on God's good earth is more glorious than
   this: to be a mother?

                    —Joseph Cardinal Mindszenty

⟨ 1 ⟩
A MOTHER'S CALL
TO HOLINESS

Holiness is not a luxury for a few,
but a duty for us all.
—St. Teresa of Calcutta

A call to holiness for me? Can that be true? What kind of holiness? Catholic mothers may not even be aware that they are indeed called to a life of holiness. Child-rearing for the most part is typically viewed as a secular role rather than a spiritual one in many areas around the globe. After all, a mother's days are overflowing with the very ordinary family activities that keep a mom engrossed with the tasks at hand. Given that her schedule is very demanding, a mother may not have occasion to offer a second thought to the possibility of a call to holiness, being satisfied with just getting her family to Mass on Sundays and holy days. While this is certainly not a bad thing, Our Lord wants more of us. He beckons us to holiness. Yes, that's right—he calls us to be saints! You may laugh, but don't give up on this book just yet! Pope Francis extols us all to a life of holiness and tells us how to achieve it! He said, "We are all called to be saints. But," he continued, holiness is not "granted only to those who have the opportunity to break away from the ordinary tasks, to devote themselves to prayer." More precisely, everyone is called to holiness in their own state of life. It is within the nitty-gritty details of life—between the pots and pans, diaper changes, and car pools—that we mothers aspire to holiness, asking for graces and responding with love, even in the most difficult moments.

Pope Francis explained, "Indeed, it is by living with love and offering Christian witness in our daily tasks that we are called to become saints. . . . Always and everywhere you can become a saint, that is," he said, "by being receptive to the grace that is working in us and leads us to holiness."

I wholeheartedly recommend beginning your day with a Morning Offering prayer to the Lord. Then you know you have started out on the right foot by giving everything over to God. Here is one that you can pray:

O Jesus, through the Immaculate Heart of Mary,

I offer you my prayers, works, joys, and sufferings of this day
for all the intentions of your Sacred Heart,
in union with the Holy Sacrifice of the Mass throughout
the world,
for the salvation of souls, the reparation of sins, the reunion
of all Christians,
and, in particular, for the intentions of the Holy Father this
month.
Amen.

— 2 —

"IF YOU KNEW THE GIFT OF GOD!"

In the Gospel of John (4:10) we become aware that the mystery of prayer is revealed by the well where one goes to seek water. This Gospel tells the story of the Samaritan woman meeting her Lord Jesus at Jacob's well. In John 4:7–25 we are told about this ordinary yet extraordinary meeting. The woman wanted to fetch water for her family, and Jesus was there at the well to offer his living water to her specifically. There, beside the well, a conversation between a Samaritan woman and Our Lord Jesus Christ began.

First, we recognize that Jesus was speaking to a woman out in public, something that was unheard of for a man at that time. Second, we see that the woman was a Samaritan, and Samaritans were despised by the Jews. Yet Jesus persisted with his loving confrontation, asking the woman about her husband. The woman tried to beat around the bush and disguise her sinful life. In a matter of time, though, by God's grace, she recognized who she was actually speaking with and suddenly began to understand the deep love of her Savior and his insatiable thirst for mankind through his discourse with her. The Samaritan woman's heart was immediately transformed, and she became a missionary, running back to her village to bring the incredible holy message of Our Lord's love and living water to her people.

St. Augustine has described this remarkable and historic meeting between the Samaritan woman and Jesus in *De diversis quaestionibus octoginta tribus*, telling us that Jesus comes to meet every human being and finds us as we are drawing our water. Interpreting this scenario as one that touches us all, not just the Samaritan woman, St. Augustine explains that Jesus is the first to seek us; his request for a drink expresses his thirst for our love. He tells us that the desire that Jesus has for our love "arises from the depths of God's desire for us" (*Catechism of the Catholic Church* [hereafter called CCC], 2560). St. Augustine has explained that even though we do not realize it, "prayer is the encounter of God's thirst with ours. God thirsts that we may thirst for him" (CCC, 2560). This profound insight from St. Augustine gives us a new way to view prayer—amazingly, God thirsts for us and wants us to thirst for him! He calls us to a union with him. Let us take some time soon to ponder that incredible truth.

St. Teresa of Calcutta often spoke about how Jesus thirsts for our love. She lived her life striving to satiate his thirst by taking care of the poorest of the poor all over this planet. I was often blessed to see this remarkable holy woman in action. I have also observed the deep reverence and understanding of Our Savior's thirst in all the Missionaries of Charity sisters that I have met. The words "I Thirst" mark every Missionaries of Charity chapel throughout the world. They are painted on the wall beside the tabernacle to remind all who enter the chapel of Jesus's thirst for our love and that we need to thirst for his love in return. Perhaps busy mothers can ponder those two simple yet powerful words soon: "I Thirst."

3

IS A MOTHER'S CALL TO HOLINESS LOST IN HOUSEWORK?

When a Catholic mother becomes aware in some way that Our Lord is calling her to come closer to him, she may naturally fear that her call to holiness might have been lost at the kitchen sink or in her laundry room. She might even think that it is impossible for her to find any extra time to pray and strive for holiness. As well, a mother may be so busy with the care of her household and children that she may forget or not even realize that God, in his divine plan, has chosen her specifically to mother her children.

Each day brings us many unique challenges, as well as a variety of ordinary routines. Sometimes the routine or monotony of tasks may cause a mother to feel that nothing extraordinary is going on—at all! She's just trying to catch up with household chores and her growing, active children who fill her days to capacity. Keeping up with the many duties in the home, the care of the children, and various activities with the family usually means that women fall into bed each night thoroughly exhausted, with their next day's "to-do" list spinning around in their brains.

Time itself can seem like a luxury that is meant for others, certainly not mothers. Newborn babies have a way of keeping their mothers up all hours of the night, and toddlers are a constant whirlwind of energy, while older children require supervision and deserve attention too. A mother needs to have the proverbial "eyes at the back of her head" and extra arms and hands to complete all of her tasks, not to mention the need for additional hours in the day! Dust settles everywhere and laundry piles up much too fast, contrary to a mother's wishes. Mothers, who are trying to care for themselves, other family members, and their bustling household, yearn for a little extra sleep if there are ever a few moments to spare, and never mind finding time for extra prayer—there simply isn't any. I vividly remember when my babies were tiny and seeing commercials on television for mattresses and wishing I could just lie down and take a nap! As the family grows, so do the activities, and time becomes even scarcer. I'm sure we all agree that mothers everywhere face the dilemma of the lack of time in their "twenty-four hours a day, seven days a week" role.

With so much responsibility heaped upon a mother's shoulders, we begin to wonder how mothers who are striving for holiness can achieve a closer union with the Lord amid the hectic pace of family life. How can a mom be true to her commitment to God to raise Christian children when her days are filled to the brim? She cannot possibly neglect her children, but what if she is neglecting God in the care of them? A mother may also feel extremely conflicted trying to figure out where she can find a quiet place and the extra time for the essential prayer needed to keep her heart and soul focused on God, while she knows that her commitment to her family requires her time and effort to focus fully on them.

— 4 —

A PATHWAY OF HOLINESS

Our Lord certainly knows about a faithful mother's dilemma. After all, he is the one who placed mothers in the heart of the home where they will indeed work out their salvation and the salvation of their families. This is accomplished by the grace of God and through a mother's loving acts of selfless service. Amazing! So, let's just hang in here, knowing that Our Lord is in control and knows full well what a mother's life is all about. He will give us strength and grace, as well as the desire to come closer to him. We must ask for it, though.

Please, dear Lord, increase my faith, hope, and love.
Work through me as I mother my family. Please help me to be confident in my mothering—offering it all to you so that it will be sanctified.

What exactly is *sanctification*, and how does that work, you may wonder? And how can a mother's prayers and actions become sanctified? If we turn to Father John Hardon's *Pocket Catholic Dictionary*, we can read the definition:

Sanctification is being made holy. The first sanctification takes place at baptism, by which the love of God is infused by the Holy Spirit (Rom 5:5). Newly baptized persons are holy because the Holy Trinity begins to dwell in their souls and they are pleasing to God. The second sanctification is a lifelong process in which a person already in the state of grace grows in the possession of grace and in the likeness to God by faithfully corresponding with divine inspirations. The third sanctification takes place when a person enters heaven and becomes totally and irrevocably united with God in the beatific vision (from the Latin *sanctificare*, to make holy).

Mothers have within their power the ability to help a great deal with their family's sanctification process. When a mother who is in the state of grace faithfully prays to Our Lord and by "faithfully corresponding with divine inspirations" asks him to use all of her prayers, works, joys, and sufferings for the benefit of her family, she is laying the groundwork for the pathway of sanctity for her family—"stone by stone," prayer by prayer, action by action. Each day affords continual opportunities to truly give everything to Our Lord so that eventually our life will become a living prayer to God. Just try to imagine the cobblestone path toward heaven in your mind that you are building for your family each day within the heart of your home during your vocation of motherhood. It is a beautiful and sacred path constructed with blood (to bring forth your child's life), sweat (the arduous work in the home), and tears (of joy and of sorrow intertwined throughout our tapestry of motherhood). Your loving responses to your family members and your sacrificial commitment to serve them helps to bring the family closer and closer to heaven by way of the holy path you are forming. Okay, it's not just cobblestone. Go ahead and, with your woman's eyes, imagine the beautiful flowers too, that grow beside the path! The varied gorgeous colors and hues, the wonderful fragrant scents transformed from the blood, sweat, and tears; all lining the sacred path to heaven! Oh, and the beautiful birds swooping down and butterflies flittering around!

St. John Paul II told us in *Familiaris Consortio*, "Among the fundamental tasks of the Christian family is its ecclesial task: the family is placed at the service of the building up of the Kingdom of God in history by participating in the life and mission of the Church"(49). I imagine that if our families are to be building up the kingdom of God, we had better start thinking about our call to holiness as mothers responsible for the sanctification of our families, as well as helping to build the kingdom. We can recall Servant of God Archbishop Fulton Sheen's sentiments: "To a great extent the level of any civilization is the level of its womanhood. When a man loves a woman, he has to become worthy of her. The higher her virtue, the more noble her character, the more devoted she is to truth, justice, goodness, the more a man has to aspire to be worthy of her. The history of civilization could actually be written in terms of the level of its women."

— 5 —

PRAYER THAT ANIMATES OUR LIVES

St. Maximilian Kolbe's words are a powerful reminder to everyone about our individual calls to holiness, but I feel these words apply especially to mothers. He said, "It is for us to become holy here and now, for we cannot be certain whether we will be here this evening." While we hope to be here this evening, only Our Lord knows for sure. Mothers aspire to holiness and work at their sanctification in the "here and now"—in the nitty-gritty daily activities that overfill our days. Will we be cognizant of our present moments each day?

When a mother's heart is in the right place with the Lord—even in just wanting to please him—she will be a radiant example to her family in the heart of her home, her little domestic church. She will strive to come closer to Our Lord by increasing her prayers to him even if it can only be in little aspirations from her heart as she goes about her mothering: *"I love you, Jesus! Please give me strength to do my job well. Please bless my family. Help me to be a better and more understanding wife and mother. Please help me to selflessly bring my family to you."* Our example will radiate out toward others as well, to help with the building up of the kingdom of God that Pope John Paul II often spoke about.

We are reminded in the *Catechism*:

> Prayer is the life of the new heart. It ought to animate us at every moment. But we tend to forget him who is our life and our all. This is why the fathers of the spiritual life in the Deuteronomic and prophetic traditions insist that prayer is a remembrance of God often awakened by the memory of the heart: "We must remember God more often than we draw breath." But we cannot pray "at all times" if we do not pray at specific times, consciously willing it. These are the special times of Christian prayer, both in intensity and duration. (CCC, 2697)

Rest assured, dear mother, and believe in your heart that the selfless love you bestow upon your family in your service to them, often unnoticed, by the grace of God is transformed into a very beautiful prayer—helping to sanctify your family. Continue to offer Our Lord your heart each day, and every moment of the day, and you will be richly blessed.

SOMETHING TO PONDER

How can a mother like me aspire to holiness when housework, the care of my children and husband, and responsibilities galore overfill my days?

RECIPE FOR HOLINESS

Start with a generous dose of surrender to God's will by meeting Jesus "at the well" each day. Add a heaping Morning Offering to God of all my prayers, works, joys, and sufferings.

My thirst for holiness will be satiated by Christ's living water. As I give everything to him, my actions will be sanctified, and my life will become a living prayer.

MOTHERHOOD'S TAPESTRY

Miracles of life,
Tiny fingers and tiny toes,
Each new life unique,
Forever love,
Unending joys,
Feelings of pride,
Sleepless nights,
Warmth and hugs,
Amazing miracles,
Sacrifice and fatigue,
Tender coos, bitty sighs,
Little worries and concerns,
Belly laughs,
Growing pains,
Patient endurance,
Graces from God,

Prayer That Animates Our Lives

Pain and heartache,
Prayerful days, prayerful nights,
Bigger worries and concerns,
Answered prayers,
Peaceful heart,
Big squeeze hugs,
And much more love,
All woven together,
In motherhood's tapestry,
Not to be traded in for anything in the world!

*Dear Lord, please grant me strength, grace,
and an understanding love. Dear Jesus, I trust in You.*

THE GIFT OF A CHILD THROUGH ADOPTION

My baby is waiting
As am I for our first embrace,
My womb has been empty;
However, the womb of my heart
Has opened wide for the gift of life!
Dear Lord, please unite my adopted child with me,
According to your holy will,
So that we can establish our family
As soon as possible,
For my arms are aching for our first embrace,
By your grace to be followed with many more!

*Dear Lord, thank you for the gift of life You have given me
and for the anticipated gifts of more children
through the blessing of adoption. Amen.*

— 6 —

A BLESSED VOCATION
OF LOVE

Woman can only find herself
by giving love to others.
—Pope John Paul II, *Mulieris Dignitatem*

Let's talk about love—God's love. "God is love, and he who abides in love abides in God, and God abides in him." We know these familiar words from the First Letter of John (4:6). Pope Emeritus Benedict XVI also used these words to open his first encyclical, *Deus Caritas Est.* He told us: "These words from the First Letter of John express with remarkable clarity the heart of the Christian faith: the Christian image of God and the resulting image of mankind and its destiny. In the same verse, St. John also offers a kind of summary of the Christian life: 'We have come to know and to believe in the love God has for us.'"

St. John Paul II spoke about love again in his Apostolic Exhortation *Familiaris Consortio*:

God created man in his own image and likeness: calling him to existence through love. God is love and in himself he lives a mystery of personal loving communion. Creating the human race in his own image and continually keeping it in being, God inscribed in the humanity of man and woman the vocation, and thus the capacity and responsibility, of love and communion. Love is therefore the fundamental and innate vocation of every human being. (11)

Motherhood is truly a vocation of love. Love is the driving force, the essential power at the heart of this very sublime vocation. Mothers come to know and to believe in the love that God has for them through the encounters with God and his love each and every day in the midst of their families. He is there: present in our homes, in our laundry rooms, at our kitchen tables, and truly living within every aspect of our domestic churches. Many graces are bestowed upon mothers within their lofty and loving vocation. This doesn't mean that because God is there with us then everyone in our domestic church has a sparkling halo hovering over their heads or our family resembles a page out of *Butler's Lives of the Saints*! Maybe far from it! Every family is a work in progress.

"I have produced a man with the help of the LORD" (Gen. 4:1 NRSVCE). Our Lord makes his love for us mothers evident by the fact that he actually forms a partnership with us and our husbands and permits human life to be created within us! An unfathomable mystery and miracle! I wonder how anyone can doubt the miracles of God's love when we can look into the eyes of our children and of children everywhere and see with remarkable clarity that God has indeed created these individual and unique human beings.

"Woman can only find herself by giving love to others," we have learned from St. John Paul II (*Mulieris Dignitatem*, 30). A woman will find herself within her motherly vocation, where she is a living spring of love. The love found within the role of a mother is undeniably reaffirmed each time she feels her child's embrace and experiences the great affection of her heart for them. Other times, her endless love transcends the difficulties and struggles along the way in raising her children. We can be assured without a doubt that God has put mothers in the heart of the home where they indeed work out their salvation and the salvation of their children.

We can experience our vocation as a tapestry of absolute and utter joy intertwined with the sacrifice, challenges, and suffering that a mother is called to endure for the love of her children. Whether it means putting aside our own desires, enduring an uncomfortable pregnancy, experiencing the pain of childbirth, or bearing heartache in one form or another—a mother's love encompasses it all.

— 7 —

MOTHERS ARE HEROES TO
THEIR FAMILIES!

A mother is called by God to practice the *heroic virtues*. You may wonder why this is necessary, or perhaps you may wish it were not! We are human, after all, and may not feel inclined to embrace suffering nor want to work harder than we must. We often feel tired or worn down from sleepless nights in the care of the family. Couldn't a mother get by with a mediocre or half-hearted acceptance of Our Lord's call to her? No. It's not possible, because the very nature of a mother's work in the home and family is in dealing with the human person and is sacrificial in its very fundamental nature and essence. Wouldn't you agree? Just bringing your child into the world is a huge sacrifice in itself, even though we are not thinking of the sacrifice when we are holding our bundles of joy. And yes, it is one of the most beautiful events that can ever occur in life, yet in order for it to take place, a mother must experience pain and discomfort. It's a fact of life that we can't ignore or dismiss. And as a mother continues to care for this child whom she has given birth to or who was handed to her in adoption, she also experiences other pains and discomforts throughout her daily life in the home.

Let's talk about heroic virtues. Looking again to the *Pocket Catholic Dictionary*, we learn:

> Heroic virtue is the performance of extraordinary virtuous actions with readiness and over a period of time. The moral virtues are exercised with ease, while faith, hope, and charity are practiced to an eminent degree. The presence of such virtues is required by the Church as the first step toward canonization. The person who has practiced heroic virtue is declared to be Venerable, and is called a "Servant of God."

A mother practices the heroic virtues when she faithfully and selflessly devotes her life to the rearing of her family in a way that is pleasing to God. Her everyday duties and acts of selfless love in the household are the "extraordinary virtuous actions" that Father John Hardon, SJ, spoke of. Recalling Mother Teresa's words about us all being called to sanctity, we also see that it is within these heroic actions that a person grows in holiness—to one day be declared "Venerable" and a "Servant of God."

Incidentally, I had the great privilege of knowing and learning from Father Hardon, as he was my spiritual director for a number of years and also my daughter Mary-Catherine's godfather. He spoke to me often about the heroic virtues, as well as the fact that there is a lot of evangelization work to be done in our world. He is now deceased and considered a "Servant of God." The cause for his canonization is currently being investigated. To be around Father Hardon was to be around holiness—it emanated from him. A day does not go by when I don't call upon him for his intercession. I always knew that he was right up there on the level of Mother Teresa, and I was very humbled and joyfully grateful to know him as I did. Father Hardon was also instrumental in helping Mother Teresa found the contemplative branch of the Missionaries of Charity sisters, and he gave the Missionaries of Charity nuns the benefit of his holy wisdom through the many retreats he offered at their convents and through a study course he designed for them at the request of the Holy See.

St. John Paul the Great highly encouraged mothers in their vocation of raising their little saints to heaven throughout their joys and sufferings. He was quick to point out the sacred mission of mothers. I particularly like his words, "The silent but effective and eloquent witness of all those brave mothers who devote themselves to their own family without reserve, who suffer in giving birth to their children and who are ready to make every effort, to face any sacrifice, in order to pass on to them the best of themselves" (*Evangelium Vitae*, 86).

If those words don't make you feel like a hero to your family, as well as give you added courage and strength for the journey ahead, I'm not sure what will!

8

A MOTHER'S VALUE

St. John Paul II spoke about a woman's family role compared to all other professions. He said:

> There can be no doubt that the equal dignity and responsibility of men and women fully justifies women's access to public functions. On the other hand, the true advancement of women requires that clear recognition be given to the value of their maternal and family role, by comparison with all other professions. Furthermore, these roles and professions should be harmoniously combined, if we wish the evolution of society and culture to be truly and fully human.

He went on to say:

> The mentality which honors women more for their work outside the home than for their work within the family must be overcome. This requires that men should truly esteem and love women with total respect for their personal dignity, and that society would create and develop conditions favoring work in the home.
>
> With due respect to the different vocations of men and women, the Church must in her own life promote as far as

possible their equality of rights and dignity; and this for the good of all, the family, the Church and society.

But clearly, all of this does not mean for women a renunciation of their femininity or an imitation of the male role, but the fullness of true feminine humanity or outside of it, without cultures in this sphere.

Unfortunately, the Christian message about the dignity of women is contradicted by that persistent mentality, which considers the human being not as a person but as a thing, as an object of trade, at the service of selfish interest and mere pleasure; the first victims of this mentality are women.

(*Familiaris Consortio*, 23)

To make matters worse, in addition to this contradiction of women's dignity by our culture's mentality that St. John Paul II spoke of, as I mentioned earlier, we live in a society where, sadly, a woman's value is most times measured by the size of her paycheck or lack of one. If a mom decides to devote her time to her family's care without pursuing outside employment, she may be considered less significant or inferior—possibly even ignorant, I hate to say! Occasionally, it becomes very apparent that not everyone appreciates a faithful mother's devotion because of their personal issues with jealousy or their misunderstanding of a mother's sacrificial love.

I have experienced the jabs of jealousy and criticism from others at times because I was committed to raising my children full-time. Some people viewed my dedication with condescension through their professional farsightedness and at times expressed various disparaging remarks. Others would say, "Oh, it's nice that you have the luxury to stay home."

Yet I believe that it is *not* a luxury—it is a choice and a decision to do without some material things and comforts to be there for our little ones; it also requires putting aside our own aspirations for achievement in a particular field or direction. We have brought children into the world or have accepted children through adoption, and we should care for them assiduously. We don't have to have quite as big a house, a television set in every room, an extra computer, or even two vehicles. Indeed, there are those who scoff at this notion.

Of course, it is nice to have some comfort or technology available to our families, but this is not all necessary, and we can make sacrifices so that we can raise our children with our full attention and not expect day-care centers or babysitters to fulfill our obligations. We must ask ourselves if we would like our children to learn the values and beliefs, or lack thereof, of caregivers or of ourselves.

Obviously, we know that not all mothers are able to stay home full-time because they need to help support their families due to challenging situations and financial obligations. I do not wish to judge these mothers in any way, nor do I want them to feel that they are not mothering properly. I only wish to encourage all mothers to be present to their families whenever they can and for as much as possible, not giving in to a culture that dictates to them where they should find their place in this world.

Additionally, there are mothers who may hold a position as a doctor, nurse, or teacher, or who work in another capacity that serves the community. Such a mother may feel that it is difficult to leave her position of service. Nonetheless, if it is possible to do without her income so that she can be home and present to her children, this would be the very best scenario. In time, with her husband's help or with help from a relative or close friend, she can resume a position in the workplace when the children are older. A Christian mother needs to follow God and follow her heart to do what is right for her family.

— 9 —

DEMANDS FOR PERFECTION AND MIXED MESSAGES

We women today are faced with a barrage of prevailing messages from our society that supposedly promote us. Women have been told for quite some time that they should liberate themselves and become more like men to acquire certain freedoms. Many women have found that this "freedom" being offered actually strips them of their unique femininity. Unfortunately, today's women are made to feel that their home life is mundane, monotonous, and uninteresting. Supposedly, women should be chasing after better, more meaningful achievements outside the home. It's no wonder that so many women today are feeling confused, misdirected, exhausted, or depressed—trying to figure out their roles, feeling compelled to accomplish more and more, trying to prove their worth or fulfill their desire to feel more appreciated. They can become quite exhausted seeking an impossible perfection while striving to fit in with society's expectations.

Women have been put through the mill, so to speak. However, as Christian mothers, we can consider the fact that nothing can be more meaningful than to be part of the creation of a human being, to be able to nurture it within our bodies, and then raise our child within a loving home—preparing him or her for eternal life. In my opinion, nothing compares—nothing! This realization can help stop some of the searching of our restless souls. Our awareness of this mission—to be responsible for human life—can calm all our fears and uncertainty, helping us to focus on the gift of our vocations.

St. John Paul II so tenderly and brilliantly spoke to women in *Mulieris Dignitatem*, "On the Dignity and Vocation of Women." This apostolic letter that he penned in 1988 speaks to women of every state of life and was the first apostolic letter written exclusively for women.

In it, he tells us:

A woman is strong because of her awareness of this entrusting, strong because of the fact that God "entrusts the human being to her," always and in every way, even in the situations of social discrimination in which she may find herself. This awareness and this fundamental vocation speak to women of the dignity which they receive from God himself, and this makes them "strong" and strengthens their vocation. Thus, the perfect woman (cf. Prov. 31:10) becomes an irreplaceable support and source of spiritual strength for other people, who perceive the great energies of her spirit. These perfect women are owed much by their families, and sometimes by whole nations.

(*Mulieris Dignitatem,* 30, emphasis added).

Reading John Paul II's poignant and profound words, we can find renewed strength and a realization of our God-given purpose within our vocations of sacrifice and love. But, I believe that we need to pause and ponder the fact that women have been entrusted with the human being. Wow! As well, can we seek to become more aware of this entrusting as St. John Paul II underscores? It is when we are "aware" of this entrusting that we become "strong."

— 10 —

CAUGHT IN THE SNARES OF THE DEVIL

Women can sometimes be blinded by the devil's tactics and innocently become victims because of the persistent mentality in today's culture. Women may buy into culture's false promises and allurements, hoping that they are moving in the right directions.

We need to be aware that the devil, the prince of darkness and trickery who never sleeps, will stop at nothing to destroy the family—the primary vital cell of society that was given by God himself. These may seem to be scary words, but let's not be deceived. Therefore, it is important for mothers to stay close to Our Lord through prayer and follow their hearts and God-given intuition to live out their vocation of motherhood with love.

Mothers must bear in mind that love is never a mere feeling, but something far more valuable. It is a dedication and a decision to live a life that unquestionably requires sacrifice and commitment. The deep satisfaction and joy that comes to a faithful mother who sacrifices herself for her family is absolutely incomparable to any other reward she may ever experience in life. Dear mothers, please do not allow the culture to direct your mothering.

Let us heed St. John Paul the Great's profound message to women, "Mary's words at the Annunciation, 'Let it be done to me according to your word,' signify the woman's readiness for the gift of self and her readiness to accept a new life" (*Mulieris Dignitatem*, 18).

When a mother responds with a wholehearted "yes" to life, choosing to care for her children attentively, lovingly, and selflessly, her children's requirements will be met with unconditional love that will absolutely steady them on the narrow path, preparing them for life ahead.

SOMETHING TO PONDER

How can I find myself through my vocation of mothering?

RECIPE FOR A BLESSED VOCATION OF LOVE

Mix equal parts prayer to Our Lord for the graces needed to perform the heroic virtues within my household and awareness of the mission God has entrusted to me. I will find myself by giving love to others.

A MOTHER'S HEART

A mother's heart
Is love and tenderness personified,
Expanding in response to each new life
That it is asked to receive.
Yielding, bending,
Opening wider still,
Enduring sacrifice,
Stretching,
Embracing joy,
Giving without measure,
Unconditional love,
Forever.
Thank you, Lord, for the gift of a mother's heart!

ONE MORNING

Breakfast and dishes, children dressed,
Out the door and off to school,
Little ones playing underfoot,
Floors being swept, dishes put away,
Children to love,
Prayers need to be said.
Pages to color and books to read,
Towers need building, flowers watering,
Menus to plan, food to buy, errands to run,

Children to care for,
Prayers need to be said.
The baby needs nursing, diapers need changing,
Clothes to wash and fold and press,
Little faces to wash and kiss,
Children to serve,
Prayers need to be said.
Bellies to tickle,
Babies to coddle,
Children to guide,
And give a listening heart,
Prayers have been said.
Sigh.

Dear Jesus, please give me strength.
Thank you for allowing me to see
the incredible significance in a mother's love
and how my acts of service to my family
are very real prayers to you. Amen.

— 11 —
A Gift of Self

*A woman's dignity is closely connected
with the love which she receives by the very
reason of her femininity; it is likewise connected
with the love which she gives in return.*
—St. John Paul II, *Mulieris Dignitatem*

From the moment a woman conceives, she is given the gift of a child as she reciprocally gives the gift of herself to her child and to her family. Even though we know without a doubt that motherhood is by far one of the most rewarding vocations, at the same time we recognize that it is when a mother becomes selfless, fully dedicating her life to her child, that her child will be raised with extraordinary and unconditional love, receiving the most invaluable gift ever.

"The Creator grants the parents the gift of a child. On the woman's part, this fact is linked in a special way to 'a sincere gift of self'" (St. John Paul II, *Mulieris Dignitatem*, 18). A mother can care for her child according to what our world considers acceptable, while she is absorbed with her own comforts and pursuits. Or she can truly and deeply love her child, wanting much more for him or her—wanting only the best. She will put her own interests aside for a while and be totally present to the little soul that Our Lord has entrusted to her care. This donating of self is very doable when a mother desires what God wants for her child. The sacrifices of her time will be well worth the efforts as she watches her children grow in love and grace.

Speaking about donating of self, the words that St. John Paul II left us moms are so very encouraging and affirming, acknowledging our heroic vocation in his encyclical *Evangelium Vitae*. He described a mother's devotion and her heroism, saying, "The silent but effective and eloquent witness of all those brave mothers who devote themselves to their own family without reserve, who suffer in giving birth to their children and who are ready to make any effort, to face any sacrifice, in order to pass on to the best of themselves"(86). Words like these from such a saintly leader can only help to inspire us, reminding us that we can be virtuous mothers, continuing to put one foot in front of the other heroically, giving the best of ourselves each day during our journey throughout motherhood.

— 12 —
A CHILD IS BORN

*Sacred Scripture and the Church's traditional
practice see in large families a sign of God's
blessing and the parent's generosity.*
—Catechism of the Catholic Church, 237

Let's consider how a child comes into being. Isn't it true that it is really without his or her consent? He or she comes into this world in a state of total vulnerability after residing and growing for nine months within the mother's womb. Just as the baby depended on the mother to answer yes to its life and to make the proper choices of food, nutrition, rest, and exercise during her pregnancy, the baby is also thoroughly dependent upon others for survival outside the womb. Isn't it up to us to care for that child with the utmost respect, concern, and love? As a child grows, he or she is just as dependent on the parents for love and guidance. Pope Emeritus Benedict XVI said, "From their conception, children have the right to a father and mother to take care of them and accompany them as they grow."

From *Familiaris Consortio* we learn, "By fostering and exercising a tender and strong concern for every child that comes into this world, the Church fulfills a fundamental mission: for she is called upon to reveal and put forward anew in history the example and the commandment of Christ the Lord, who placed the child at the heart of the Kingdom of God: 'Let the children come to me, and do not hinder them; for to such belongs the kingdom of heaven'" (26).

We can pray that every baby will be able to experience the love of being cuddled in his or her mother's loving arms, feeling her warm embrace and tender attention, which will give him or her necessary protection and love that he or she deserves for a happy beginning to life. Let us pray that mothers' hearts will respond to their new children with a selfless and pure devotion.

Tired mothers may at times feel that their efforts and service to their families are more than a bit overwhelming. They can sometimes dwell on the challenging situations, feeling that this present moment they are enduring is the way it will always be—nothing will change. They become absorbed in it and perhaps obsess over it and may be unable to have any vision for the future. They are deep in the "trenches," so to speak. I have heard many a complaint from new mothers trying to adjust and juggle the sometimes overwhelming responsibilities in the home.

When I encounter these mothers, I truly wish I could convey to them just how fast life has a way of speeding by. I want them to be able to enjoy that part of their mothering before it is too late and they regret that they wished it away. Mothers should be aware of this fact so that as they are immersed in the nitty-gritty details of caring for their babies and small children—during the sometimes unpleasant or unappreciated tasks—they will stop and reflect and realize that it truly all has a divine purpose. They can then grab hold of the moment and savor it before it passes them by.

Moreover, the passing of time also reminds us to be patient with our "little" duties and our difficult ones, aware that "this too shall pass" when we face the everyday challenges that beset us. We can be confident knowing that after we have fulfilled this piece of our mothering, we will soon be on to another phase—another season. Each moment is important. For our children's sakes, let's try not to wish them away.

Let us mothers take heart in St. John Paul II's words, "May mothers, young women, and girls not listen to those who tell them that working a secular job, succeeding in a secular profession, is more important than the vocation of giving life and caring for this life as mother." We mothers can do our part to combat the mentality of our society that attempts to convince women that they are only as valuable as their paycheck. We can make our point best with our living example—that motherhood is a high calling and a most sublime vocation and privilege.

As Pope Emeritus Benedict XVI once said:

God entrusts to women and to men, according to the characteristics that are proper to each, a specific vocation in the mission of the Church and in the world. I think here of the family, community of love, open to life, fundamental cell of society. In it, woman and man, thanks to the gift of maternity and paternity, together play an irreplaceable role in regard to life. From the moment of conception, children have a right to count on a father and mother who care for them and accompany them in their growth. The state, for its part, must sustain with adequate social policies all that which promotes the stability of matrimony, the dignity and the responsibility of the husband and wife, their rights and irreplaceable duty to educate their children. Moreover, it is necessary that it be made possible for the woman to cooperate in the building-up of society, appreciating her typical "feminine genius."

SOMETHING TO PONDER
How can I recognize a divine purpose in my mothering?

RECIPE FOR CREATING A GIFT OF SELF

I will turn a deaf ear to those who attempt to convince me that something else is more important than the "vocation of giving life and caring for this life as mother" (St. John Paul II), and I will combine this with lots of prayer to recognize God's unique purpose for me.

A CRY FOR YOUR LOVE
Your beloved little one
Who was once warm and cradled within your womb,
Being rocked by your every movement,
Now cries for your love and comfort.
He has emerged into a most different world.
He needs your caress and your soothing voice,
The warmth of your body against his.
Look into the eyes of your child and speak to him often.
He needs your comforting voice,
He has heard it from inside your womb.
He needs your arms around him, your presence,
Your unconditional motherly love,
To carry him through his entire life.

Blessed Mother Mary, St. Anne, and St. Gerard Majella,
please pray for us.

THROUGH A CHILD'S EYES
A mother's hand is warm and secure to hold;
Her shoulder is soft to rest a little head upon.
Her voice is steady, consoling, and encouraging.
Her embrace is like no other,
Melting away every fear or frustration,
Chasing away every hurt.
She is forever ready to answer the unremitting questions

Asked by her inquiring youth with their saucer eyes.
She strives to keep everyone in peace and harmony
As she continues to balance the scales of home life.
She attempts to fill every need,
Stretching herself beyond measure.
And her smile never fails to warm the hearts of her children.

O Mary, conceived without sin, pray for us who have recourse to thee.
O Mother Mary, pray for us so we may imitate your virtues
as a mother
and love as you loved.

— 13 —
CARVING OUT TIME
FOR PRAYER

*Prayer is the life of the new heart. It ought
to animate us at every moment.*
—Catechism of the Catholic Church, 2697

"It should never be forgotten that prayer constitutes an essential part of Christian life, understood in its fullness and centrality. Indeed, prayer is an important part of our very humanity: it is 'the first expression of man's inner truth, the first condition for authentic freedom of spirit,'" as we learn from St. John Paul II in *Familiaris Consortio*, (62).

Many of the saints have told us that it is critical to find time and quiet in which to pray. St. Edith Stein, also known as Teresa Benedicta of the Cross, said, "The only essential is that one finds, first of all, a quiet corner in which one can communicate with God as though there were nothing else, and that must be done daily. . . . One is to consider oneself totally an instrument, especially with regard to the abilities one uses to perform one's special tasks. . . . We are to see them as something used, not by us, but by God in us."

A dedicated and faithful mother soon learns that for the happiness and health of her family and to really survive in our world today, she must work out a plan for prayer for herself and her family. However, since her life is filled with the care of her family and concerns for her children and husband, she soon discovers that it is crucial to offer her busy life to the Lord and really every moment of the day to him. She can turn to the Lord when she opens her eyes to a new day, each day, offering her heart and her day totally over to the Lord. She offers him in advance the ordinariness of her days—her joys, her acts of loving service, doing the laundry, cleaning the toilet, feeding the baby, and refereeing the children, as well as her prayers, her sufferings, and sacrifices. She can be assured, without a doubt, that her day will then have started off with the right approach and disposition. She can ask for all the grace and strength required to aid her on her journey so that she may guide her children well.

A mom asks Our Lord to use her this day as his instrument, so that her children and others in the family may see him in her and be drawn to Jesus. By offering her day first thing in the morning in her own prayers or the words of the Morning Offering, God will certainly bless a mother's day, craziness and all! She can then be assured that he is in control and knows her busyness with the children and her household.

— 14 —

PRAYING IN
THE DOMESTIC CHURCH

*It is good to be devout as a housewife but
sometimes you need to leave God at the altar
to find him at home.*
—St. Frances of Rome

"The Christian home is the place where children receive the
first proclamation of the faith. For this reason, the family
home is rightly called 'the domestic church, a community of
grace and prayer, a school of human virtues and of Christian
charity," as we learn from the *Catechism* (1666). Additionally,
Pope Emeritus Benedict XVI tells us, "Every home is called to
become a 'domestic church' in which family life is completely
centered on the lordship of Christ and the love of husband
and wife mirrors the mystery of Christ's love for the Church,
his Bride."

There are many seasons in a mother's life. When our
children are young, we are sometimes housebound with
their care—we do our praying for the most part within our

"domestic church." As the children grow, we find ourselves out and about in the community involved with their activities. We can find more opportunities at times to stop in for a quick respite before the Blessed Sacrament where Our Lord awaits us. As we accompany our children to their various activities and outings at the library, at museums, on playdates with other families, or on trips to the grocery store, we can hope and pray that our influence and example to others in the community will be of help to their souls as we are mothering our children.

Throughout the various seasons, we mothers continue to minister to the needs of others as we live out our busy role as the mother to our family, that unique unit of people that God has brought together. Even when our children have grown into adults, we continue to pray for them within our "domestic church," delighting in the times we will continue to share with them when they come back to the nest to visit us alone and when they are with their own families.

The busyness of our motherly vocation may cause us to fear that we cannot be as prayerful as we should. However, we need to remind ourselves that Our Lord certainly knows about our lives. After all, isn't he the one who has put us in this place, the heart of the home, as mother to our children?

Our Lord sees our hearts. He hears our pleas. He knows our desires to come to him more fully, without reserve. He does not want us to kneel down to pray and in the process to neglect our children who are depending on us. That's an instance when that form of prayer would actually be wrong.

We can and should encourage our children to pray with us, but when that isn't possible, we have to be happy with what our Lord gives us, believing that he knows what is best for us all. Mother Teresa used to say that, "We must give what He takes and take what He gives with a smile. Can we give that smile to him?"

A mother's prayer is truly prayed throughout her countless loving, sometimes unnoticed, tasks within her "domestic church." Many graces are merited there, right in the heart of our homes. Miracles are actually worked in human hearts because of our devotion and faithfulness to our vocation! Our lives become a beautiful prayer.

And yes, of course, we never stop looking for a special time and place for prayer in which to meet Our Lord because we know that is essential for our family's spiritual growth. But we must be patient with what God gives us. We may want to be at Mass, Adoration of the Blessed Sacrament, or a Bible study on a particular day, but because our child is sick, we need to remain home caring for them. That is where we should be—staying home, taking care of our needs and the needs of our families, praying throughout our loving responsibilities. Our Lord wants us to meet him right where we are, as we are "drawing our water" in the here and now of our lives.

At times, we may set aside a special prayer time in which we hope to have at least a few quiet moments of spiritual reading and meditation. We prepare to meet with Our Lord: kneeling, hands clasped, ready to pray—and suddenly our toddler runs in after waking up early from a nap, fully energized and in need of our immediate attention. Or at times a distraught relative calls on the phone at that moment. Or a neighbor shows up at our door needing someone to talk to. There should be no concerns about lost time with Jesus because our arranged prayer time was interrupted. We serve God in our children and in others. Our Lord hears our prayers from the depths of our hearts as we thank him for our lives, our families, and the blessing of caring for them.

Our holy Mother Church provides prayer guidelines through offering the faithful specific rhythms of praying with the intention of nourishing continual prayer. The *Catechism* states, "Some are daily, such as morning and evening prayer, grace before meals, the Liturgy of the Hours. Sundays, centered on the Eucharist, are kept holy primarily by prayer. The cycle of the liturgical year and its great feasts are also basic rhythms of the Christian's life of prayer" (CCC, 2698).

We each have our own unique journeys of prayer—as unique as our families are. As mothers, we weave prayer into our lives and into the lives of our families, always setting the example for prayer. We express it through Christian tradition's three major forms of prayer: vocal, meditative, and contemplative. To learn more about what our Church teaches about prayer, I urge you to read Part Four of the *Catechism*: Christian Prayer.

— 15 —

TEACHING OUR
CHILDREN TO PRAY

The *Catechism* teaches us that we must be the first and foremost educator of the faith to our children. A faithful mother knows that it is essential to develop not only her own prayer life, but her family's prayer life, and also to teach her children to develop their own individual prayer lives. Christian mothers need to be faithful to their personal prayer, strive to put aside time for family prayer, and impress upon their children that they are also called by God to be prayerful people. A mom will remind her family about the blessings in remaining close to Jesus and his Blessed Mother at all times.

Because she realizes the importance of instilling a prayer life within her children, a mom teaches her children to follow her own example—to pray. She begins this fundamental aspect of raising her children when they are just infants as she prays in their presence, all the while lovingly teaching them the necessity of turning to prayer at all times. A mom begins teaching the building blocks of prayer when her children are still in her womb, praying for them as they grow within her. A baby is surely nourished by these prayers, as Our Lord bestows many graces on a prayerful mother's child.

As our children grow, they will begin to understand the prayers said in their presence—little aspirations voiced out loud, thanking God for a new day and his many blessings. At other times, we sit or kneel with our little ones, teaching them to bless themselves, fold their hands, and communicate with the Lord. We want them to know that they can speak from their heart to a loving God at any time. We don't want them to feel forced into prayer by using a regimented approach. We won't turn them away from prayer if we show them that it is a natural, beautiful, and loving conversation. We will be laying a critical foundation for them, teaching by our own example that prayer is something to look forward to and treasure. We can remind and encourage our children throughout the day to offer their hearts to God from time to time, letting Our Lord know that we love him. These are simple but vital teachings. Wherever life takes our "little ones" down the road, we can feel comforted knowing that they were raised with prayer and they will surely turn to prayer throughout their lives, even at the times when it may not seem as obvious to us parents.

The *Catechism* tells us, "The Christian family is the first place of education in prayer. Based on the sacrament of marriage, the family is the 'domestic church' where God's children learn to pray 'as the Church' and to persevere in prayer. For young children, in particular, daily family prayer is the first witness of the Church's living memory as awakened patiently by the Holy Spirit" (CCC, 2685).

— 16 —

HELPING OUR FAMILY TO BE UNITED IN PRAYER

Where does love begin? In our homes.
When does it begin? When we pray together.
The family that prays together stays together.
—St. Teresa of Calcutta

St. John Paul II often preached about the importance of family prayer: "Only by praying together with their children can a father and mother penetrate the innermost depths of their children's hearts and leave an impression that the future events in their lives will not be able to efface" (*Familiaris Consortio*, Nov. 22,1981). We may wonder how we can pray as a family, especially when getting everyone together can be as impossible as keeping vegetable oil from dancing off a hot griddle when its gets spattered with water. Just the words "prayer time" can cause the kids to quickly get lost in other pursuits—*very* quickly, I might add! They suddenly have very important things to do! Therefore, in addition to raising my kids with prayer when they were very young so that it became a natural family event, I also included prayer with our mealtimes when we were together already. This worked well for us. (And because I want to help other families, I have recently written a book titled *Feeding Your Family's Soul: Dinner Table Spirituality*, to aid parents and grandparents in transforming an ordinary mealtime into a celebration of and teaching of the Faith.)

If you haven't yet begun the practice of family prayer in your own households, you can start right now by praying just one Hail Mary at the dinner table with your crew after grace has been said, to keep your family united in prayer while beseeching our Blessed Mother for her help for your family. You may want to pray an Our Father as well. I have always found this to be an ideal time and place, because each family member is usually present, as well as pretty hungry! Eventually, you can increase to three Hail Marys, and before too long you might be able get a decade in at the dinner table, either daily or weekly.

Praying the family Rosary keeps us in loving communion and puts us under the protective mantle of our dear Mother Mary. She will grant us the graces we need to be faithful to family prayer and bring us close to her Son. Let's not forget to ask her! The Blessed Mother has been given the power by God to "crush the head of the serpent," the devil. Let's make use of that powerful treasure for our families. We should call upon Mary often through our decades of the Rosary or aspirations to her at any time of the day or night.

Morning prayers can be said kneeling by the side of the bed or at the breakfast table. Sometimes my family's morning prayers were said on the run! As I was backing the car out of the driveway to get to the bus stop with my children after a crazy, rushed morning, we blessed ourselves, began a prayer to our guardian angels, and said an Our Father, a Hail Mary, and a Glory Be. We thanked God for a new day in which to serve him in others, we voiced our intentions for our sick friends and relatives, and we asked Our Lord to use us this day to spread his love to others. He hears our prayers even when we are rushed!

At calmer moments, mothers may have the opportunity to bring their children to daily Mass or for visits to the Blessed Sacrament where Jesus awaits us. When out on errands or traveling to activities with our children, we can occasionally stop at the church to make a visit. We can tell our children about Our Lord's great love for us, and how very pleased he is when we take a bit of time out of our day to come to him in the Blessed Sacrament, where he gives us his peace and graces.

The *Catechism* gives examples of favorable places for prayer:

> The church, the house of God, is the proper place for the liturgical prayer of the parish community. It is also the privileged place for adoration of the real presence of Christ in the Blessed Sacrament. The choice of a favorable place is not a matter of indifference for true prayer.

For personal prayer, this can be a "prayer corner" with the Sacred Scriptures and icons, in order to be there, in secret, before our Father (Matt. 6:6). In a Christian family, this kind of little oratory fosters prayer in common. (CCC, 2691)

A PRAYER CORNER

Setting up a prayer table or a prayer corner in a family room, den, library, dining room, or living room in your domestic church is a good way to keep the children focused on the blessed and holy rather than the secular. In the next chapter I will tell you about how my grandmother's holy images around her home made an unforgettable impact on my heart. We mothers can also make a lasting impression on our children—and later our grandchildren—by creating an atmosphere of prayer in quiet ways and examples, as well as in more tangible ways.

To set up a prayer corner, you only need to place a small table in a designated area. You may place statues on the table or framed holy pictures above the table. You may have a basket or bowl of rosary beads handy on the table, and prayer cards or prayer books in a basket under the table or on top. Your prayer area will be "kid-friendly," and it will grow as they grow. You can use big, colorful, wooden rosary beads and Christian and Catholic picture storybooks, saints' books, and the Bible. You can provide a kneeler, pillows to kneel or sit on, little chairs— or simply just use the table. The kids can get involved, too, by drawing pictures of Jesus, the Blessed Mother, the saints, or the Holy Family, which can be hung above the table.

This area will help to inspire passersby to stop for a quick prayer or at least serve as a reminder to them of the necessity of prayer. When family members and visitors see the holy images, they will be prompted interiorly to pray—kind of like a prayerful subliminal message! This area can be used to gather the family for prayer at designated times and can also be used individually. It can also serve as a welcome place to come and listen to a Bible story or saints' story before bedtime. Let the Holy Spirit inspire you about how to utilize your prayer corner.

Other ideal opportunities to fit prayer into a family's busy schedule are while traveling to various activities or on family trips. Praying decades of the Rosary and other prayers and petitions voiced as a family can be achieved easily while you are all together. Another type of prayer that we can teach our family is to offer up the illnesses, little sufferings, or inconveniences that they endure; asking Our Lord to use these little sufferings or pains for the souls in purgatory. Remember that phrase, "Offer it up"? Well, it's not to make light of someone's suffering but to encourage them to make use of it! St. Teresa of Calcutta used to say, "A family that prays together, stays together."

— 17 —

TURNING TO
OUR BLESSED MOTHER

*Indeed, while leading a life common to us,
one filled with family concerns and labors,
Mary was always intimately united to
Christ, furthering the work of the Savior.*
—The Decree on the Apostolate of the Laity

A faithful mother learns to call upon the Blessed Mother often. She mothered Jesus and really wants to mother us too! She was human like us, and although she was the mother of Jesus, she also needed to be faithful with her prayer life. She experienced the joys and sorrows of motherhood like any other mother, so she knows what it's all about. She knows about prayer and about the care of the family. She can teach us to find a balance between the two to bring us peace in our vocation. Mary can bring us closer to her Son, Jesus. Let's ask her!

We know that our dear late Holy Father, St. John Paul II, had a much-cherished relationship with the Blessed Mother. He called upon the Blessed Mother at all times. He lived his life under her mantle and said that it was Mary who kept the bullet from killing him that was fired at him during the assassination attempt.

St. Mother Teresa of Calcutta, who was very dear to St. John Paul II, told me on a number of occasions to call upon the Blessed Mother for help, strength, and safety. She taught me a simple but powerful prayer, "Mary, Mother of Jesus, be Mother to me now." Mother Teresa prayed the Rosary often throughout the day and instructed the sisters, priests, and brothers to do the same.

While we know that we will never accomplish what our Blessed Mother has, or come close to her holiness, we too as mothers are called to holiness in the sublime role of raising our children. Mary has demonstrated so many attributes and virtues for us to emulate in our vocation as a mother. We can look to Mary and realize that her deep faith was really the foundation of her holiness. We should remember that Mary was human like us and needed to pray so that she would be unwavering in her faith, just as we mothers are called to do. Mary's faith is the same gift available to us. We can ask Mary to be a mother to us and guide us closer to her Son, Jesus.

Mothers can indeed learn from Mary, who is an example of one who listened to God and allowed the Holy Spirit to inspire and guide her. We learn from Mary that a mother's prayer is powerful. When we are asked to endure suffering or pain within our vocation, we can turn our thoughts to Mother Mary and ask her assistance and intercession. Throughout difficulties, trusting in God during particular situations within their home life, mothers can meditate on Mary's faithful trust in Our Lord and in the guidance from the Holy Spirit. When we experience the deep joy within our role as a mother, we can feel an affinity with someone who has also experienced deep joy in mothering Jesus.

Mary's marvelous "yes" to God indeed changed the entire world for all eternity. May all faithful mothers also courageously answer Our Lord, "Be it done unto me according to thy word," as they strive to raise their families in a cenacle of prayer that they have fostered in the heart of their homes.

THE ROSARY: ANCIENT BUT EVER NEW

Praying the Rosary, a Catholic devotion, dates back to the Middle Ages. By reciting the prayers of the Rosary and meditating on the various mysteries, one comes closer to Jesus and Mary through prayer and meditation. The Rosary is said to be a powerful weapon against evil. It is a perfect prayer for Catholic families. We learn from St. John Paul II in *Familiaris Consortio*:

> There is no doubt that the rosary should be considered as one of the best and most efficacious prayers in common that the Christian family is invited to recite. We like to think, and sincerely hope, that when the family gathering becomes a time of prayer the rosary is a frequent and favored manner of praying. In this way, authentic devotion to Mary, which finds expression in sincere love and generous imitation of the Blessed Virgin's interior spiritual attitude, constitutes a

special instrument for nourishing loving communion in the family and for developing conjugal and family spirituality. For she who is the Mother of Christ and the Church, is in a special way, the Mother of Christian families, of domestic Churches. (61)

It may seem daunting to consider that the Rosary may be a form of prayer suitable for a busy mom or her family. After all, the Rosary is five decades long. A complete Rosary used to be actually fifteen decades! But with St. John Paul II's addition of the "luminous mysteries," which he introduced to us in his 2002 apostolic letter *Rosarium Virginis Mariae*, we have an even longer Rosary with additional beautiful aspects of Our Lord and his Blessed Mother's lives to meditate upon. Should we just give up the idea of fitting the Rosary into our schedule right now? No, I don't think so. Let's call to mind once again that Our Lord is very loving and also extremely smart! He knows we are busy moms. So what can we do to heed Pope John Paul II's words about the special nourishment and loving communion as well as lots of good graces that we will receive by saying the Rosary?

Since Our Lord is an understanding God, he will listen to our Rosaries in bits and pieces. Busy mothers can find time to squeeze in decades throughout their days. I like to say at least one decade for my children's safety while they are traveling to school or work in the morning. Depending on my schedule that particular day, if time permits, I continue with the Rosary at that time. If not, I pick up the Rosary at my next opportunity and finish it throughout the day. I have to admit, my ten fingers come in handy (no pun intended) for decades of the Rosary. Many times I pray the Rosary without rosary beads—sometimes I marvel that my fingertips aren't worn off from the constant use while counting my Hail Marys as I pray the Rosary throughout my days! I also make sure that my husband, Dave, and I get a Rosary prayed together each day. After all, Our Lady of Fatima who appeared to three shepherd children, St. Francisco, St. Jacinta, and Lucia, has requested that we pray a daily Rosary for peace in the world, for sinners, and for reparation. Let's teach the children the Rosary while they are young. Try to get your husband on board with the Rosary, too, if possible. Trust me! This may take time to develop. Be patient and prayerful.

Mothers can pray decades of the Rosary while nursing a baby, in the quiet moments while getting a child down for a nap, or while folding laundry, traveling in the car, or taking a walk, to name some instances. I've said many a Hail Mary in front of my clothes dryer, folding my family's laundry.

This reminds me of the time when my son Joseph asked me in the morning when he was leaving for school if I would please pray for him that day. He had a number of important events scheduled and welcomed some extra prayers. I always pray for my children at every opportunity, but when my child asks specifically, I jump right on it! So there I was, folding laundry and offering all of my Hail Marys at the dryer for Joseph. After praying so often in my laundry room, I don't think it's possible for me to fold laundry without thinking of my family and praying for them. There are many graces attached to our work! We can pray through everything! Our lives become a prayer that is very pleasing to Our Lord.

As mothers, let's remember to offer our hearts to Our Lord often throughout our busy days. Our *Catechism* reminds us: "Prayer is the raising of one's mind and heart to God or the requesting of good things from God" (CCC, 2559).

Prayer is a gift! I am convinced of God's tender love for mothers because he has put us in a position in the family—in the heart of the home—in which we will be constantly beseeching him for his help and guidance, conversing with him frequently as we are raising our children.

SOMETHING TO PONDER

How can I teach my family to pray as a family, when attempting to gather them together for prayer is almost as impossible as keeping hot oil from dancing off a hot skillet when it gets spattered with water?

RECIPE FOR CARVING OUT TIME FOR PRAYER

I will foster a strong belief that it is of utmost importance and an awesome responsibility to set the tone for prayer in my household, to set the example, and to lovingly guide my family in prayer so that prayer will become to them as natural as breathing. Incorporating family prayer throughout our daily routines and gatherings and decorating my domestic church with sacred images will draw my family to the holy rather than the secular.

LOVE FOR LAUNDRY: FOLDING HAIL MARYS
Laundry: a never-ending task,
Looming over me, growing beside me,
Requiring my time and lots of energy.
How can a mother embrace this job?
Quietly, I pray.
Folding my family's clothes,
I think of them and of you, Lord,
Thankful for this blessing:
The awesome privilege of caring for them!

*Dear Lord, please grant me all of the graces I need
to see the hidden treasure in housework
and in caring for my family!*

RADIANT FLAME
Beside the tabernacle
The flame on the candle flickers
In the red glass holder
Announcing your presence, Jesus.
I cannot be there with you, Lord, to drink in your graces
and love.
Instead, here I am drinking in your graces
In my domestic church
While the flame burns in my heart
Announcing your presence, Lord.
Thank you, Lord, for your love!

— 18 —

UNFORGETTABLE
TEACHINGS

*The best and surest way to learn the love of
Jesus is through the family.*
—St. Teresa of Calcutta

I remember vividly kneeling down on the floor with my
siblings and my mother at home as the beads of our rosaries
glided through our fingers while we prayed the family Rosary
together at various times as I grew up. My mother would light
a candle in a small, blue votive glass holder that she set in
front of a statue of the Blessed Virgin Mary. We all knelt with
her and prayed the beautiful prayer of the Rosary together.
My mother especially drew us together on holy days and
during the months of May and October in Mary's honor or
when a relative was sick and in need of prayer, always placing
us under the protection and mantle of Mary. I will be the first
to admit that we did not always act as if we had sparkling
halos hovering above our heads! Most times we did not! Even
so, learning the Rosary was a foundational part of my faith
journey. Although at the time I didn't realize the importance

of this family prayer—asking for Mary's intercession—the details of this form of family prayer are etched on my heart and remain with me.

My father worked very long hours to support our large family of eight children and was usually asleep very early each night to be up and starting all over again at four o'clock in the morning, commuting an hour to his job. He also had physical challenges and needed his rest. Therefore, my mother took on the responsibility of leading her children on the path of holiness and keeping us on the straight and narrow. My mother must have acquired her steadfast faith and her devotion to the Blessed Mother from her own very faithful and prayerful mother who taught her so well.

Speaking of my grandmother—walking into my grandmother's apartment was like entering a church. She had a holy water font on the wall by her front doorway and pictures of Jesus, Mary, Joseph, and the saints covering every available space on her walls. She also placed the image of her hero, Pope John Paul II, in every room. She was Polish, after all! Her love for him was obvious and contagious! Rosary beads could be found anywhere and everywhere in her little home, along with many holy statues. I think she might have even had holy pictures in the bathroom!

If you were going to visit Grandma, you were going to visit Jesus, Mary, Joseph, and all the saints too! I bet strangers who came to her door and were eventually invited in were amazed at her display of faith and perhaps even touched by it. We were quite accustomed to it—it was part of the tapestry of our lives; Grandma was a holy woman indeed. We were fortunate to have the benefit of her many Rosaries prayed for her entire family.

Her love and value for her very large family was documented in the massive photo albums stacked all throughout her home. I can safely say that two things Grandma would never be without were her Rosary beads and her Brownie camera! (For you young folks, a Brownie camera is an old-fashioned camera—actually Kodak's *first* handheld camera.) We Coopers and all our cousins, aunts, and uncles were very familiar with the fact that Grandma took photos of everything and everyone—mostly everyone! We knew we couldn't escape it, so we may as well accept it and try to have a sense of humor about it. Truth be told, I have acquired Grandma's habit of taking pictures of all my kids and now my grandchildren! I just tell everyone that they will be happy later on that I captured all of those things for posterity's sake!

Thank goodness that my grandmother captured our youth in the hundreds upon hundreds of photos she took with her old, but dependable, camera. Otherwise we wouldn't have much to show for all those years that seem to have disappeared in a flash before our eyes; we might not be able to conjure up our memories without them. Nowadays, my own children and my siblings laugh when I bring the camera out and snap away. They had better get used to it because I don't plan on stopping anytime soon, God willing!

My mother bringing her children together to pray the Rosary and family prayers, and my grandmother's very obvious display of her Catholic faith as well as her prayerful advice for all of her children and grandchildren, left deep impressions on the entire family. How could they not? We were so fortunate to be raised with the Catholic faith.

We too can raise our families with prayer and traditions of the kinds of family prayer we participate in together, whether we are happily married Catholic women, single Catholic mothers, or Catholic mothers whose husbands are not praying so much. These prayerful times will remain in our children's hearts as they navigate life one day on their own and as they are raising their own children.

St. John Vianney shared some beautiful sentiments about decorating the home with holy things. He said, "To decorate the houses with religious pictures is a custom as old as Christianity itself, for the true Christian has always considered his home as nothing less than a temple of God, and the religious pictures as means to extend and preserve the spirit of Christianity in the home."

— 19 —

YOU KNEW
IT WAS SUNDAY

Observe the Sabbath day, to keep it holy.
—Deuteronomy 5:12

Growing up in a large Catholic family was celebrated in the ordinariness of our lives. We had our routines, chores, chickens and pets to care for, and of course, our Sunday dinners. Back when I was a little girl, we didn't have a Saturday night vigil Mass. We always knew when it was Sunday because we went to Mass in the morning, usually enjoyed pancakes with bacon and eggs for breakfast, and then often visited relatives or invited them to our house.

My siblings and I were always expected to be home for Sunday dinner, which was served midafternoon. It didn't matter what event you were invited to or what else was going on. When it was Sunday, you were home at two o'clock in the afternoon for a big Sunday family meal together. It was a very rare occasion that you were let off the hook.

We enjoyed a simpler meal together later in the day too. It was an extra treat when some of our relatives would drop by. We kicked back a bit and enjoyed the day. It was a day of rest, but this was not exactly true for my mother, because she worked hard to put out a nice spread on the table for all of us. I rarely saw my mother sit down except at mealtimes or when the day was finished. We all pitched in by setting and clearing the table and helping with the dishes, but looking back I now realize that my mother without a doubt had her two feet firmly planted in the heart of our home in her 24/7 role.

My mother provided a wonderful tradition for her eight children and my father for family Sundays. It seemed so ordinary and natural for us growing up—that was the beauty of it, really. Now, being a mother myself, I see such richness and profound meaning to Sundays in the family. Life in the domestic church is a blessing to be cherished.

The third commandment tells us (actually commands us) to keep the Lord's Day or *Sabbath* holy. The *Catechism* tells us that Sundays are a day designated for the celebration of the Sunday Eucharist, rest, and time with family: "Just as 'God rested on the seventh day from all his work which he had done,' human life has a rhythm of work and rest. The institution of the Lord's Day helps everyone enjoy adequate rest and leisure to cultivate their familial, cultural, social, and religious lives" (CCC, 2184).

I also love this explanation from the *Catechism* about the appropriateness for rest on a Sunday and for also allowing others to rest: "God's action is the model for human action. If God 'rested and was refreshed' on the seventh day, man ought to 'rest' and should let others, especially the poor, 'be refreshed.' The Sabbath brings everyday work to a halt and provides a respite. It is a day to protest against the servitude of work and the worship of money" (CCC, 2172).

These days, though, it's tough to tell one day from another at times. We are so busy that we often carry our busyness into Sundays too. It's challenging not to do this, however, when it seems like there's so much to do and so little time! Are we doing too much? Do we need to plan a bit better?

What's a Christian mother to do? How do we observe the Sabbath when we are catching up on laundry, washing the kitchen floor (because we didn't have a chance to do it on Saturday and it's disgusting), and endless other household tasks, as well as trips to the store for materials for a school project, or for our kids just wanting to shop?

We have to draw the line somewhere and then stick with that. Perhaps it will be in vowing not to do laundry on a Sunday, in refusing to go to stores unnecessarily, and certainly in choosing to spend more family time together, as well as making sure everyone knows that they are all required to be present for Sunday dinner. Of course, we know that some sports events have crept into our Sundays, so perhaps we need to adjust our schedules at times. However, it is up to us as parents to set the limits and lay the foundations—for instance, never compromising by skipping Mass due to an activity or an overfilled Sunday. The traditions we begin now will be carried out throughout our family's life to a certain extent and even into our children's future family's traditions.

We should also ask ourselves how we can slow down a little, and what we can do to enjoy a day of rest.

Perhaps you can try some of these suggestions:

1. Vow to make certain adjustments to your Sunday schedule.
   * A regular dinnertime when everyone is required to be present
   * Little or no shopping
   * No laundry or heavy cleaning
   * Adjusting activities in any area to achieve more calmness
   * Hug your kids and spouse
   * Hug them again
   * And again (Now wasn't that nice?)
2. Read a book.
3. Read to the kids.
4. Take a nap (or daydream about the possibility).
5. Do something outside together.
6. Do some yard work together (even though it's technically work, it can be fun and recreational!).
7. Take a walk in the fresh air, weather permitting.
8. Tell a story while walking.
9. Tell jokes.
10. Play a board game.
11. Talk to the family about something inspirational (the lives of the saints, perhaps).
12. Pray.
13. Prepare dinner together.

14. Bake or make a dessert together.
15. Call a relative you have been meaning to talk to but haven't had time.
16. Invite a relative over for a visit.
17. Give the dog a bath (or maybe not).
18. Write a letter or card (not an email) that you will mail to brighten someone's day.
19. Have the kids write a thank-you note to someone special in their lives to express how grateful they feel to know this person or how much they appreciate that person.
20. Dedicate a specific time to do nothing but ponder and meditate. That's right, schedule a period of "nothing"! But try not to fill it with technology.
21. Plan an outing—possibly to a shrine, a basilica, or a pilgrimage site.
22. Get creative; draw some pictures or do a craft with the kids.
23. Start a new tradition with the kids.
24. Think about what you can do to help a needy family in the upcoming holidays.
25. Smile!
26. Smile some more—be happy that God has truly blessed you!

You get the idea—and you can come up with your own ways to make Sundays special.

Sadly today, Sundays in most places are just another day of the week. Many people have given up on going to

Mass because they are too busy and cannot seem to fit an hour with Our Lord into their packed schedules. Scores of Catholic families have chosen to attend the five o'clock vigil Mass on a Saturday night every single weekend. This vigil Mass was established so that if one could not go to Mass on Sunday, there was another option in the case of health workers, police officers, and people who had to work on Sundays. Saturday evening Mass was granted by Pope Paul VI (as part of the reforms of the Second Vatican Council), who in April 1969 promulgated the apostolic constitution *Missale Romanum*, which outlined the changes to the liturgy and gave the effective date to be the first Sunday of Advent in 1969. There may be some who sincerely believe that by going to the Saturday vigil Mass they are *extending* their Sabbath for more rest and family time. In this case, far be it from me to seem as if I am criticizing their choice—that is not my intent.

Vigils used to be a time prior to a feast day or solemnity in which to offer special prayers and fasting. The *Pocket Catholic Dictionary* defines "vigil" as:

> the day or eve before a more or less prominent feast or solemnity. It was observed as a preparation for the following day with special offices and prayers and formerly with a fast, honoring the particular mystery of religion or the saint to be venerated on the feast day. The Church today observes solemn vigils for Christmas, Easter, and Pentecost. Although a number of such solemn vigils has been reduced

since the Second Vatican Council, the Church still wants the notion of vigils to be kept alive in the minds of the faithful. Thus "it is fitting that Bible services on the vigils of great feasts, on certain ferial days of Lent and Advent, on Sundays and feast days, should also have the same structure as the liturgy of the Word at Mass."

It has become an overly convenient occurrence to go to Mass on Saturday night, I think, rather than get up on a Sunday morning to go to Mass. I have attended many vigil Masses where the prevailing atmosphere was extremely casual, and I got the feeling that the attitude of some who were present (wearing their extremely casual clothes) was, "Quick, let's get this obligation out of the way so that we can get on with our weekend!" I'm sorry if I sound judgmental because I sincerely do not want to be. I'm just reporting what I have seen and experienced. It's particularly sad to see people practically running out of the church before the final blessing. Of course, I am not stating that everyone who attends the vigil Mass shouldn't be there. I only wish to point out that the sacredness of the Sabbath seems to be sadly disappearing. Many of us are in too much of a rush to get through Mass and are very preoccupied with our weekend distractions.

Sunday becomes just another day to be filled with shopping and various secular activities that do not surround the family hearth and that do not give rest to the mind or soul. It indeed makes sense that there should be a day to ponder, pray, rest, and have meaningful time together as a family. Too much work and no rest causes undue stress and strain. However, I do realize that with so much technology available to us, we are immersed in a whirlwind of noisy activity most of the time and cannot find a quiet place to rest our weary brains! Nonetheless, mothers can try to keep things down to a dull roar on Sundays, so to speak, so that we can hear ourselves think and hear each other as well. We can encourage our children to have a bit of quiet time alone to pray on Sundays and listen to what God has to say to them. How about considering unplugging totally on Sundays? Or at least for a period of time—no gadgets or devices, no television, no videos. You might be amazed to find that when you start to be able to hear yourself think and have more time for prayer and meditation (even amid family busyness), you grow in holiness.

"On Sundays and other holy days of obligation the faithful are bound . . . to abstain from those labors and business concerns which impede the worship to be rendered to God, the joy which is proper to the Lord's Day, or the proper relaxation of mind and body" (*Codex Juris Canonici*, 1247).

I have continued my mother's tradition of serving hearty Sunday breakfasts for the brood. However, I skip the bacon (or use fake bacon) and make eggs and whole-grain pancakes instead, occasionally with some ground flaxseed thrown in. No one knows about the healthy ingredients—let's keep that as our little secret! I try to sneak good nutrition into my cooking whenever I can. I have also attempted to keep Sundays distinctive with special dinners and desserts. No matter what their ages, my kids enjoy cooking and offer their culinary skills in the kitchen. Because they do, our kitchen is usually humming with lots of activity, laughter, and even singing at times, especially from one daughter in particular—which makes for another fun part of our occasions of coming together as a family.

Now that my children are living on their own, I am deeply in my glory when all of my "ducklings" are in a row—home and together for dinner. We always reminisce and break out in laughter as we gather in the kitchen around the center island, checking out new recipes from laptops or cookbooks, making a mess while adding ingredients to the meals that we are preparing in the heart of our home. Who cares about the mess? Not me, that's for sure! Now a grandmother, I am in my glory when my grandsons Shepherd and Leo come over to visit and we hang out together!

It's so important to lead countercultural lives in order to survive in our Faith these days. So much of the culture continually pulls at us to embrace a different way of life—so contrary to our beliefs. Servant of God Archbishop Fulton Sheen pointed out that "dead bodies float downstream" and that "it takes a live body to resist the current." We don't want to be a dead body and go with the flow of our culture! Let's vow to bring back the holiness of Sundays to our families.

The celebration of Mass is paramount, of course, as is our time together. We should not rely on the vigil Mass on a regular basis; rather, we should go to church on Sunday when it's possible. There will be sports games, practices, school projects, and various activities that will inevitably fill our Sunday schedules, and it is important to support our children in their endeavors. We just have to keep watch over the schedules to be sure that they don't take over our lives. Let's determine to have a nice Sunday dinner where everyone is expected to be present.

I know many a Christian family whose grown children have left the Church to search on their own while perhaps still respecting the family's Sunday traditions of the family meal and time spent together. So, while your older ones may have deserted Mother Church for a time, you can always hang on to hope, remain consistent with your prayers for them, and continue with the other family members to set the example of Sunday Mass together, meals together, and time together. Sadly, some older children may not care too much for the family scene at all, feeling a need to be more independent. Not to worry, though—the impression, reality, and blessedness of their Christian family will remain in their hearts and will also help to draw them back to the Church one day. Even if your older ones who live away from home don't participate with you at all for a time, they have the comfort of knowing that you are still there, still carrying on the traditions of their childhood, and that you will welcome them with open arms when they are ready. Sundays together are powerful examples for our families and for society.

Getting back to the dinner table—there are many temptations for kids to quickly run off after dinner to do their own thing. Let's try to sit together, however, for a few extra moments at least, to relish our family time. Parents need to preserve the sacredness of the dinner table, breaking bread together in the blessedness of the family, and bearing in mind, too, that all our dinners together will not be Norman Rockwell picture-perfect. Perhaps even far from it! At times, there will be spills and occasional outbursts and overtired, cranky little ones. However, dinnertime is a moment to be together and reap the benefits.

I have found through all my years of mothering that time speeds by awfully quickly, and I want to encourage you to savor and enjoy your times together too. Let's also stay connected with relatives nearby, whenever possible utilizing the Lord's Day as a day to enjoy the company of extended family as well. There is nothing like grandparents or aunts and uncles and cousins mingling with the family and creating wonderful memories together.

─ 20 ─

AN ATMOSPHERE OF
LOVE AND PRAYER

I love how St. Teresa of Calcutta encouraged us to pray. "Love to pray—feel often during the day the need for prayer, and take trouble to pray. Prayer enlarges the heart until it is capable of containing God's gift of himself. Ask and seek, and your heart will grow big enough to receive him and keep him as your own." As we set the example in the household for prayer, our children will pick up our cues and strive to be prayerful themselves. According to Mother Teresa, our faithful hearts will enlarge to contain God!

Earlier in this book I mentioned St. John Paul II's words, "Only by praying together with their children can a father and mother penetrate the innermost depths of their children's hearts and leave an impression that the future events in their lives will not be able to efface." These profound words deserve repeating here, helping us to understand why the family tradition of prayer in the home will be a truly unforgettable teaching tool that nothing along the road in the future can efface. The combination of prayer and sacred images throughout our homes will help to inspire the soul.

We mothers must purposefully create an atmosphere of love, prayer, and joy in which to raise our families. That responsibility rests firmly on our shoulders. Family traditions play a huge part in our children's upbringing and will be what is etched upon their hearts—creating memories to take with them into their lives ahead.

In addition to the prayerful atmosphere that we strive to create in our households, we also want to provide a sense of love, peace, happiness, and security within our domestic churches. As wives and mothers, we work at our relationships with our husbands, displaying our affection for one another freely, appropriately, and openly so that our children feel loved and secure within the sacred walls of our domestic churches. Household displays of affection are wonderful and necessary for a healthy family. We also keep a united front with our husbands when it comes to establishing rules and parameters for our children—another way to keep them feeling secure and on the right path.

Let's not forget about fun and games with our children! After all, our bustling household isn't only about chores and housework. We take delight in all the enjoyable stuff too! It's great to allow for some time to play with our children, getting right down on the floor to get involved with their activities. The children always appreciate it when Mom takes a break from what she is doing to play a board game with them or some other activity where everyone can have a good, wholesome, fun time. I certainly understand how difficult it can be to break away from our duties in the household to pause for refreshment with the children; however, it is not only good—it's necessary! Go outside and draw on the driveway with sidewalk chalk, take the kids on an outing, go for a walk out in the fresh air, go to the library, visit with some friends, stop by the church to visit Jesus in the Blessed Sacrament, and then go out for an ice cream cone—the possibilities are endless! And don't feel guilty about it! Time speeds by, and we want to enjoy our children and allow them the time to be with us.

I remember when I was a little girl drying dishes after dinner each evening while my mother washed. I never thought about it being a painful or annoying chore. I actually enjoyed it because I was doing something with my mother. I was always bursting at the seams to let my mother in on the latest clues I had discovered in the many adventures of the Nancy Drew books that I was reading at that time. She listened intently while I chattered away to her. She seemed very interested in my recounting the stories. In no time, the dishes were all clean, dried, and put away. There were other times when—in between the Nancy Drew talk—I could casually insert something that was on my mind. It was my mother's and my time to talk as she passed the clean dishes to me, and I dried them and put them away.

Don't be afraid to get your kids involved with the household chores. You can make it personal by investing time in your conversations with them while you are busy with your tasks. As a mother, I have found that sometimes it is much easier to have a discussion about an important or sensitive topic while doing something side by side rather than face-to-face with our children. Children are also more apt to open up to us while we are spending time with them while out on a walk, doing dishes, cooking together, or involved in doing something together, so that they won't be squirming in their chair, feeling uncomfortable and avoiding eye contact with us.

Let's be sure to find time to converse with our children throughout our busy days, showing a sincere interest in their lives and letting them know that we will always be nearby to help or simply just to listen. We help to create unforgettable memories and teachings that will remain etched upon their hearts forever.

SOMETHING TO PONDER

How can I get my family to spend more time together and treat Sundays as the Lord's Day?

RECIPE FOR A SAVORY BROTH OF
UNFORGETTABLE TEACHINGS

I set the tone in my home for Sundays, and I also set the parameters and expectations for my family regarding Mass and Sunday dinner: by not planning unnecessary shopping trips, by fostering an atmosphere of rest and fun with friends and relatives, and by hopefully even finding a quiet time to ponder and pray.

MY HEART IS KNEELING WHILE MY HANDS ARE MOTHERING

Dear Lord, my hands are required
To care for my little ones—
I cannot fold them now in prayer.
My mind needs to focus
On the task at hand with my children,
Since they are in need of my help.
I know you will understand
That I am not able to kneel at this moment,
Although I want to be with you.
Please accept my heart
To kneel before you
As my hands are mothering my children.

Dear Lord, I thank you for this incredible gift of motherhood!

— 21 —

THE HEART OF
THE MATTER

*"With Christians, a poetical view of things
is a duty. We are bid to color all things
with hues of faith, to see a divine meaning
in every event."*
—Cardinal John Henry Newman

All Christian women are entrusted with a mission. We may not all realize it or be aware that we are being called to it, but it is true! Mothers particularly are called to an incredible mission. Let's take a look at what St. John Paul II had to say about our mission. He said, "The moral and spiritual strength of a woman is joined to her awareness that *God entrusts the human being to her in a special way.* Of course, God entrusts every human being to each and every other human being. But this entrusting concerns women in a special way—precisely by reason of their femininity—and this in a particular way determines their vocation" (*Mulieris Dignitatem*, 30). He went on to explain that the moral force of women was expressed through a great number of women in the Old Testament, at the time when Jesus walked on this earth, and in later ages up to the present day. These women drew their strength from the awareness of their entrusted mission. *Awareness* is powerful.

I am reminded of St. Teresa of Calcutta, who was a saint of our era and who drew strength from the awareness of her mission to care for the poorest of the poor. Because she was aware that Our Lord was calling her to serve him in the poorest of the poor, she had strength to put one foot in front of the other each day to serve him in them—even when she didn't *feel* Our Lord's call or his presence or *hear* his voice any longer as she experienced a "dark night of the soul." Mother Teresa was granted the graces to walk in faith to do God's work. However, it was necessary for her to *decide* to act upon these graces. The same graces are also given to all women if they ask for them and if they accept them. Our Lord has a plan for each and every one of us women. Perhaps we need to wake up from our slumber and recognize that we too have a mission from God and we should accept his graces!

Before we broach that topic about our personal missions, let's think about the women in the Gospels who made a powerful impact because they listened to Our Lord's calling. St. John Paul II was sure to mention the women in the Gospel in his apostolic letter to women, *Mulieris Dignitatem.* Of course, there is Mary, the Mother of God, who made everything else possible with her courageous "Yes." St. John Paul II also pointed to many other women in the Bible of various ages and conditions. Some of these women were crippled with illnesses and were later healed by Jesus. Others sought Jesus out, asking his help for family members and others. Because of graces flowing and Jesus's healing hand, many of the women were transformed and decided to follow him. They accompanied the apostles and Jesus through the villages, proclaiming the Good News of the kingdom of God.

We also see that women were mentioned in the parables. As we read the Bible and also Church documents and letters such as *Mulieris Dignitatem*, we recognize the fact that Jesus was loving to women—always, thereby transcending his own culture. He treated women with great love and tenderness and was an amazing promoter of women's dignity. "Christ speaks to women about the things of God, and they understand them; there is a true resonance of mind and heart, a response of faith" *(Mulieris Dignitatem*, 15).

Of course, we are also well aware that women were the first witnesses of the Resurrection. St. John Paul II said:

> From the beginning of Christ's mission, women show to him and to his mystery a special *sensitivity which is characteristic* of their *femininity.* It must also be said that this is especially confirmed in the Paschal Mystery, not only at the Cross but also at the dawn of the Resurrection. The women *are the first at the tomb.*
>
> They are the first to find it empty. They are the first to hear: "He is not here. *He has risen,* as he said" (Matt. 28:6). They are the first to embrace his feet

(cf. Matt. 28:9). They are also the first to be called to
announce this truth to the Apostles (cf. Matt. 28:1–10;
Lk. 24:8–11). The Gospel of John (cf. also Mk. 16:9)
emphasizes *the special role of Mary Magdalene.* She is the
first to meet the risen Christ. . . . Hence she came to be
called "the apostle of the Apostles." Mary Magdalene
was the first eyewitness of the Risen Christ, and for this
reason she was also *the first to bear witness to him before the
Apostles.* This event, in a sense, crowns all that has been
said previously about Christ entrusting divine truths to
women as well as men. (*Mulieris Dignitatem,* 16)

Meditating upon the fact that Jesus was always tender
and loving to women and has entrusted them with great
missions and callings, we can be sure that he is calling us
too. Women are at the heart of our world. We certainly
recognize a woman's place in the heart of the home.
Women have been given many gifts and privileges by God.
Unfortunately, we know that throughout history, women
have often been pushed to the margins of society and
considered to be inferior.

The radical sexual revolution of the 1960s—which
supposedly was meant to promote women—in actuality
caused further damage to women's souls, their dignity, and
their bodies. It offered women "freedom" to become more
like men, and later in 1973 that "freedom" would also allow
them to murder their own children in their wombs and get

away with it, when abortion was legalized by the United States Supreme Court! Women bought into this notion of acquiring "freedom" after having struggled throughout the years without such freedoms. However, look where it took us—look where we are now. There are countless wounded women and millions upon millions of innocent dead babies. I'm sorry to sound so blunt; however, it is a very sad and real fact.

Fifty years ago, in 1968, just a few short years before abortion was legalized in the United States, Pope Paul VI released his encyclical *Humanae Vitae* (On the Regulation of Human Life), which reaffirmed our Church's teachings against artificial methods of birth control and proclaimed Mother Church's unwavering position in defense of all aspects of the sanctity of human life. *Humanae Vitae* transcends our world's turbulence and turmoil and continues to speak today of the respect for the marital union and the family, and the utmost respect for the dignity of all human life from conception until natural death. We must not allow the persistent "throwaway" mentality of our culture to cloud our minds or cause us to think that *Humanae Vitae* is an old-fashioned discourse. It is more relevant today than ever. We must apply it to our lives and be an example of our Church's teachings so that other mothers and women who are struggling to understand or accept Church teaching may be edified by our lives. I highly encourage all to download a copy of it from the Vatican website or buy a copy from a Catholic bookstore.

Earlier, I spoke about a woman's mission and her awareness of God's entrusting the human being to her, using St. John Paul II's eloquent words, *"God entrusts the human being to her in a special way."* A woman is given a role to care for others, specifically because she is a woman, because she is feminine. Femininity is a beautiful thing! Radical feminism is not so. Women have to realize that from their femininity will blossom many graces and blessings for society and for their families. Attempting to change a woman into a man does nothing but confuse matters and destroys the family in the process.

As we pray to Our Lord and seek intercession and wisdom from his Blessed Mother, we will better understand our authentic femininity and our missions as mothers. Biological and adoptive mothers are given the gift of the human being to nurture and love. St. Edith Stein said, "Woman's soul is fashioned to be a shelter in which other souls may unfold. Both spiritual companionship and spiritual motherliness are not limited to the physical spouse and mother relationships, but they extend to all people with whom woman comes into contact."

Obviously, not all women are mothers; however, they can be *mothers* to others in their midst because women are given motherly hearts. I know many women who are not mothers but who are mothers to so many around them. An example is my friend Teresa Tomeo, a radio host with whom I share a radio segment, "Mom's Corner," on her show "Catholic Connection" on Ave Maria Radio (and aired through EWTN), who speaks from the heart to countless people. She is aware of her mission from God and takes responsibility for it by not mincing words. She offers the truth to those willing to listen. Thankfully, even in this day of mixed messages and confusion in our culture, there are many who do listen, who want to be taught the truth or have it reaffirmed to them so that they can pick up their cross each day to follow Jesus.

My friend Mary Catherine Williams is a Catholic woman, whom I met through my website and blogs, who mothers others around her at her job as a nurse in a Catholic hospital. She offers her motherly heart and prayers to wounded police officers; young, injured car-accident victims; mothers of premature, vulnerable babies; and so many more. She gives them holy cards, medals, and spiritual books. She has been given a mission to care with her motherly heart and spread the Good News. She is a mother to others by using her God-given womanly gifts. What is your mission? It's something to think about and pray about.

St. John Paul II encourages us with his words,

A woman is strong because of her awareness of this entrusting, strong because of the fact that God entrusts the human being to her. Always, and in every way, even in the situations of social discrimination in which she may find herself. This awareness and this fundamental vocation speak to women of the dignity which they receive from God himself, and this makes them "strong" and

strengthens their vocation. Thus the "perfect woman"
(cf. Prov. 31:10) becomes an irreplaceable support
and source of spiritual strength for other people,
who perceive the great energies of her spirit. These
"perfect women" are owed much by their families, and
sometimes by whole nations. (*Mulieris Dignitatem*, 30)

I don't know about you, but I can stop right here and
relish those words. St. John Paul II, like Our Lord, always
uplifted the dignity of women and extolled them for their
God-given gifts and motherly hearts! We should strive to
pass this awareness on to other women and do our part
to raise the dignity of women and mothers. We can ask
ourselves these questions: Are we following Our Lord's will
in our lives and answering him each day with a great big
"YES!" to whatever he asks of us? Are we truly allowing Our
Lord to live through us so that others can perceive the great
energies of our spirit and be drawn to him? It's never too late
to start! Christian women have been entrusted with a great
mission. Let's pray for the awareness of our missions so that
we can truly follow Christ.

SOMETHING TO PONDER

How can I discover my mission from God and better understand my authentic femininity?

RECIPE: ESSENTIAL INGREDIENTS—
THE HEART OF THE MATTER

I will give myself generous amounts of time for meditating on women in the Gospels; reading *Mulieris Dignitatem*: "On the Dignity and Vocation of Women," penned by St. John Paul II in 1988; and praying to discover my gifts and dignity in God's eyes. I'll mix in the possibility of joining a Catholic women's study group to share insights and learn more about Church teaching.

IN THE "QUIET" OF THE HOME

As some women strive to find themselves,
Closing the door behind them each morning
To the constant spills, clatter, noise,
And demands of the young ones,
I think of all they sadly miss,
Trying to prove their worth to the world.
Each day the home has its abundant share of chaos and stress,
But it's always tempered with the coos, hugs, kisses, smiles,
And warmth of our dear children.
A mother quietly and lovingly tends
To the everyday needs of her children,
Knowing that Our Lord is pleased with her
Very ordinary, sometimes unnoticed tasks
Performed with extraordinary LOVE.

*Dear Mother Mary, pray to your Son, Jesus, for us, please,
to increase the love in our hearts for our families.*

— 22 —
THE GRACE OF
THE PRESENT MOMENT

For everything there is a season, and a time
for every matter under heaven.
—Ecclesiastes 3:1

I wonder how much of our life is taken up with lamenting about our yesterdays and worrying about our tomorrows. Naturally we want to feel secure in our lives and try to prepare for the future—it's the responsible thing to do, after all. Yet we shouldn't get so caught up with what is to come, or what has already happened, that we neglect to stay still and live right in the present moment to embrace it for all it's worth. This is certainly a challenge for most mothers because we live in a world of technology that can be very engaging and totally distracting. It is also a world that draws us to want more and more and never be satisfied with what we already possess.

St. Teresa of Calcutta often preached that in our fast-paced world, people are often in a great rush—not taking time for others. Sadly, this problem exists in home life too when the family doesn't take time for one another. As the heart of the home, we mothers need to be sure that we help our families to pause and slow down at least a little bit so that we can enjoy one another's company and be able to be open to the love from our family members so that we can also give back love in return. It's essential to establish times for family togetherness, whether it be lingering at the dinner table to converse, enjoying a family outing, working together in a soup kitchen, or watching a movie together: our time together is sacred and indispensable. We need to give our personal gift of time to our husband and our children. I really feel that *time* is a genuine and very loving gift since it is hard to grab hold of and is something that we seem to be lacking in our extremely busy lives and therefore difficult to part with.

When we slow down and give of our time, we are truly giving of ourselves. Yes, housework can loom over us and needs to be done, yet it will always be there to pick up from where we left off. Truly giving of ourselves can be accomplished in so many ways, including giving a listening ear to one who desperately needs solace, comfort, or companionship. We can stop folding the laundry for a few moments so that we can truly look into our children's eyes when they are in need of our attention. My daughter Mary-Catherine made this clear to me one day when she was a little girl. She said, "Mommy! Turn your face here!" I was beside her in the living room all along conversing with her while I folded a batch of clean laundry as she played nearby. But she wanted my undivided attention for a few moments. I stopped and sat her on my lap for a nice little conversation and cuddling. The laundry could wait.

We can also take a break from housework to make a phone call to a relative in a nursing home or a neighbor who lives alone. Our days seem to pass right by during our busyness, and we may find ourselves going to bed, lamenting and asking ourselves where the day disappeared to. We have to grab hold of the present moment and make the time to give time. This sounds paradoxical—however, it's very true. In a greater way, giving the gift of time is putting aside our own desires in order to raise our children with the utmost attention and love—being present to them and giving them the best of ourselves in a sometimes unfriendly and impersonal world.

This reminds me of my friend Sally who told me that her college degrees are framed and hanging over her washing machine and dryer. I thought that was so fitting. This mother put aside her personal accomplishments to be present to her children. Her degrees displayed in her laundry room remind her each day that she does indeed have a brain! She tells me that sometimes, though, she wonders! However, she is extremely happy with her decision to mother her children and not pursue a career out of the home at this point in her life.

— 23 —
TOO BUSY TO HELP?

I remember so clearly a situation that happened roughly forty years ago. It was a time when my firstborn child, Justin, was a little baby. One day I had the use of a brand-new vehicle, and not being familiar with the locking mechanism, I accidentally locked my keys inside the car. When I got out of the driver's side, I shut the door behind me and went to open the back door to get Justin out of his car seat. It was locked—*all* of the doors had automatically locked! My heart sank as I looked through the closed window and saw my car keys hanging from the ignition! However, worse than seeing my keys locked in the car was seeing my baby son in his car seat and knowing that I couldn't even touch him!

What if he suddenly got upset and started to cry? How could I comfort him? How much oxygen was in the car? It's amazing how many questions can swirl around a mother's brain in less than an instant. So that Justin wouldn't be frightened, I mustered up a couple of funny faces to flash at him through the back window while I wracked my brain trying to figure out what I should do. I began to feel more and more panicked about the situation. I was a young mother—all of twenty-one at that time—whose baby was not within reach, and there was no one around to help me in that secluded parking lot. *This is definitely not a good scenario,* I thought.

I didn't want to leave my child to go for help. This was long before cell phones were invented, or at least I did not own one. After a few minutes, a nicely dressed man came walking through the small, quiet parking lot at a swift pace. I asked him if he could kindly help me, quickly explaining my dilemma. I'm sure that he must have heard the concern in my shaky voice and could see a tear in my eye as I pleaded for his assistance. Much to my dismay, the man replied, "I am late for a meeting," as he continued quickly on his way, head down, across the parking lot. I was shocked. Call me naive, but I could not believe his response and his seemingly apparent lack of compassion regarding my awful predicament.

Thankfully, I did receive help, and all ended well with my son out of the vehicle and into my arms soon afterward. I agree wholeheartedly with Mother Teresa and feel that we are a people that are in too much of a hurry. We can't stop for a minute or two to help someone in need. We are not living in the present moments of our lives but rather rushing off to the next event.

Mother Teresa once expressed her sorrow when a person died right on the street near a place where a huge meeting to seek out ways to help the poor was being conducted. Although Mother Teresa didn't have time for meetings, since she lived her life helping the poor directly in a hands-on way, she had been invited and was en route to the meeting when she discovered this person. She felt frustrated that a person died without help while people close by talked about how to help such people. Of course, we need both forms of care: planning and doing. She was a doer—a woman who very much lived in the present moment and ministered to people in a personal way. She believed that she was serving Jesus in each person she encountered, following the directives of Jesus in the Gospel of Matthew: "Just as you did it to one of the least of these who are members of the family, you did it to me" (25:40).

St. Augustine left us with a wonderful piece of wisdom through his well-known cry to Our Lord, "Our hearts were made for thee. They are restless until they rest in thee, O God." We certainly are a restless people, often searching in all of the wrong places for peace and true happiness. St. Augustine assures us of rest for our soul when we *find* Our Lord and surrender to his will. It is only then that we will have authentic and everlasting peace. Mothers can find rest when they place their trust in Our Lord. They may be tired and worn out physically and emotionally from mothering; however, their souls can find true rest and deep joy when they give everything to Our Lord and live in the here and now.

— 24 —

GOD IS AT WORK IN THE PRESENT MOMENTS OF OUR LIVES

I often marvel about how God works. He really has everything under control—most times, unbeknownst to us. Every so often he makes us aware of the movement of the Holy Spirit and how he may be working through us to inspire others. I'm thinking about a woman named Clara right now, a woman I "happened" to sit near while waiting to be seated for lunch at a restaurant. Years ago when I was "back-to-school shopping" with the kids, we decided to have lunch together at a local family restaurant. We were told that there would be about a fifteen-minute wait to be seated. Since we had time to kill, my kids, who were old enough to go off on their own, decided to go next door to the pet store to look at the puppies. I sat down in the waiting area next to a mother with her month-old baby, who was also waiting to be seated for lunch. I admired this woman's little baby, and we got to chatting. It's amazing what kinds of conversations can transpire between total strangers, especially among women. My kids sometimes give me a funny look when they see me carrying on a lengthy conversation, seemingly out of the blue, with someone I have never met before in my life. But this happens quite often, I'll admit.

During our conversation, Clara told me how she had experienced three caesarean sections and that her doctor had told her that only three caesareans are medically advised—period. I told Clara that I had five caesareans. She was totally surprised that having five caesareans was even a possibility. We talked about welcoming life, and she expressed her opposition to abortion, explaining that her doctor told her that if she conceived "too late" in life that she should abort the baby because it would have defects. It's very sad that we live in a society where human life is not valued.

After sharing and comparing notes on motherhood, we were called by the restaurant host to our respective tables. We parted with joy in our hearts, knowing that we had come together not by coincidence, but because God in his goodness had it all under control. I was very happy knowing that I had the opportunity to share with Clara the fact that I brought five children into the world through caesarean sections and lived to tell the story! Not that I shouldn't have survived, but I chose to welcome life despite all the negativity and cautionary warnings not to do so (the medical profession is terrified of a lawsuit over the extremely unlikely chance that a uterus would rupture). Clara told me that she would like more children. She most likely will be able to have more and is now very open to that possibility.

I could write a whole book about amazing encounters in which God is so obviously at work. God is so very good and has everything under control. He arranges these encounters, such as the one I just expressed about meeting Clara by "chance." We have to be open to his whispers to our hearts and souls. I believe that it's up to all of us to offer ourselves first thing in the morning, every morning, and ask Jesus to use us at all times. We throw ourselves into his arms offering our lives to him; we give him all our prayers, works, joys, and sufferings and ask that he perfect them to be used for his glory. We ask our Blessed Mother to guide us and protect us, while bringing us closer to her Son.

— 25 —

RELISHING OUR PRESENT MOMENTS

Whatever you do in your family, for your
children, for your husband/for your wife,
you do for Jesus.
—St. Teresa of Calcutta

I love what St. John Paul II has said about patience, waiting, and interior purification. He said, "For a stalk to grow or a flower to open there must be time that cannot be forced; nine months must go by for the birth of a human child; to write a book or compose music often years must be dedicated to patient research. To find the mystery there must be patience, interior purification, silence, waiting." The time that Our Lord has given to mothers while their babies grow within them allows them time to pray and time for transformation of their hearts. This is all while the mother lives in the *present moments* of her pregnancy. It really is wonderful to have that nine-month period to pray for our unborn babies. For an adoptive mother, it is the time she waits to be able to finally take her child home to her domestic church to care for.

There are many opportunities in a mother's life in which she is busy waiting. It sounds paradoxical, doesn't it: "busy waiting"? How are we *busy* when we are *waiting*? The most perfect example is the one I just mentioned: when we are busy waiting for our unborn baby so that we can finally hold him or her in our arms. So much happens during nine months—getting the nursery ready for the baby's arrival, doctor's appointments, shopping for itty-bitty clothes—we are busy indeed! And again, adoptive mothers are also *busy waiting* and preparing for their baby to finally be released to their family so that they can begin their bonding and family times together.

There are other occasions when mothers are *busy waiting*. When our child is sick, we wait for his or her fever to go down or the coughing to stop, praying for his or her little body to heal. Walking the floors with a colicky baby, waiting patiently for our children to accomplish little feats, and waiting for our babies to start sleeping through the night, our toddlers to behave, or our teens to mature and get through their turbulent years are other times that mothers exercise a spirit of patient endurance. Through it all, we relish the time spent teaching and guiding our children ever closer to heaven.

I have to admit, though, that I happen to cherish all of the late-night feedings I experienced with each of my babies. Call me crazy to enjoy getting up in the night when I was already exhausted; however, I seriously feel that they were beautiful times of nestling and nursing. An infant wakes his or her mother in the night because his or her belly is empty and in need of nourishment. How can we feel annoyed or put out? Impossible! Yes, we are tired and in need of sleep; however, these are *present moments* of our lives that cannot be duplicated in the future. I hope that all new mothers will relish this time alone with their little infants to nurture and bond together, skin-to-skin, heart-to-heart.

I found that this quiet time at night served at least three major purposes. First, of course, it is for nourishing our infants. Second, it provides an undivided time together to bond and enjoy, which is usually exclusive since everyone else is fast asleep. Additionally, everyone will remain fast asleep when we take care of the needs of our infants—nursing and feeding our babies immediately so that they don't even have to cry to be fed. Third, it is an excellent opportunity (Our Lord knows what he is doing) to get a conversation going with Our Lord! Sometimes it seems that this is the *only* quiet time we mothers have to think and to pray. As we nurse, we can pray for our baby and our family. It can also be a time of peaceful contemplation. Many times, I have prayed decades of the Rosary, counting the Hail Marys on my fingers as my baby nursed and fell back to sleep. You can even count down the decades on your baby's fingers or toes! Sometimes, I just rested in the stillness of the quiet night, contemplating God's great love for me and my family as I nursed my baby to sleep. Nighttime feedings were a time for my baby and a time for my Lord.

God has everything all figured out. The nighttime feedings between mother and baby not only nourish the child and bring about a deep bonding, but remarkably also act as a natural child spacer, which is a form of natural family planning (NFP). Frequent and exclusive breast-feeding delays ovulation and fertility. By exclusive, I mean not supplementing with formula, juice, or water, so that there is unrestricted suckling for baby, which postpones mothers' fertility.

Speaking of patience, St. John Vianney spoke about St. Francis de Sales's patience and wonderful mastery of living in the present moment. He said, "St. Francis de Sales, that great saint, would leave off writing with the letter of a word half-formed in order to reply to an interruption." Mothers are well aware of the more than umpteen interruptions that fill their daily lives. We mothers should ask ourselves how we will respond to those "interruptions." Will it be with love? I feel that nothing is a coincidence; I believe Our Lord allows us to be *interrupted* quite often to give us unending opportunities to selflessly offer our hearts to our families and those whom he has put in our midst.

For everything there is a season,
And a time for every matter under heaven:
A time to be born, and a time to die;
A time to plant, and a time to pluck up what is planted;
A time to kill and a time to heal;
A time to break down, and a time to build up;

A time to weep, and a time to laugh;
A time to mourn, and a time to dance;
A time to throw away stones, and a time to gather stones together;
A time to embrace,
And a time to refrain from embracing;
A time to seek, and a time to lose;
A time to keep, and a time to throw away;
A time to tear. and a time to sew;
A time to keep silence, and a time to speak;
A time to love, and a time to hate;
A time for war; and a time for peace.
—Ecclesiastes 3:1–8

What can we learn from this Bible passage?

— 26 —

BEING MARTHA AND MARY
IN OUR FAMILY

Martha and Mary may be the most familiar set of sisters in the Bible. We have been told by both Luke and John that they were friends of Jesus. Luke's four-verse report has been a continual, multifaceted source of inspiration and analysis of the human heart and condition for centuries. John's account about Martha and Mary's brother, Lazarus, covers seventy verses. But what can we learn about our role as a woman in the household and our relationship with Jesus from these four short verses from Luke?

> Now as they went on their way, he entered a certain village, where a woman named Martha welcomed him into her home. She had a sister named Mary, who sat at the Lord's feet and listened to what he was saying. But Martha was distracted by her many tasks; so she came to him and asked, "Lord, do you not care that my sister has left me to do all the work by myself? Tell her then to help me." But the Lord answered her, "Martha, Martha, you are worried and distracted by many things; there is need of only one

thing. Mary has chosen the better part, which will not be taken away from her." (Lk. 10:38–42, NRSVCE)

Is Jesus rebuking Martha for not sitting at his feet? Who has made the better choice, Martha or Mary? Why would Jesus consider that shirking the responsibility of helping her sister is choosing something better? Luke's account tells us that Martha extended an invitation to Jesus to come to her home in Bethany. Luke doesn't mention Martha as having a husband but rather says that "Martha welcomed him into her home," giving us the impression that she was the head of the household. She may have lived with her sister, Mary.

We see that Martha was very concerned and possibly upset that her sister, Mary, was not helping her to prepare the dinner, and she became frustrated—frustrated enough to go to Jesus, telling him to order Mary to shape up and help her in the kitchen. Martha was even bold enough to imply that Jesus did not care about all the work that she needed to accomplish. Was Martha jealous of Mary's luxury of sitting at the feet of Jesus? Could she have been upset that Mary, along with the men, was engrossed in theological discussions while she slaved away in the kitchen? We can't blame Martha in a sense for feeling a bit overwhelmed with her duties. After all, she may have had to cook for the dozens of followers that usually accompanied Jesus. However, she was the hostess, and she had invited Jesus to her house.

Why was Mary at the feet of Jesus anyway? It could be because she was being a good hostess and had stooped to wash Jesus's feet when he came in from outdoors. She may have become engrossed and captivated in the conversation and teachings that began to ensue while washing his feet and so remained there, quietly content. When we read the Gospels, we find that Mary was often at the feet of Jesus in adoration, quietly listening—choosing "the better part." Was Jesus telling Martha that it is wrong to be in the kitchen and that she should be with Mary at his feet? I don't think so. He softly rebuked her because of her demanding attitude by saying, "Martha, Martha, you are worried and distracted by many things; there is need of only one thing. Mary has chosen the better part, which will not be taken away from her." He is not telling Martha that she was wrong in preparing the dinner or in hoping to get help in the kitchen. Rather, I believe that Jesus was explaining that it was a time in that present moment for Mary to be at his feet, and he wasn't going to take that from her just because Martha was banging pots and pans around in the kitchen and demanding that Mary help her.

Mothers have a unique role in their vocation of motherhood of being like Martha and Mary at the same time. We mothers are busy *doing* and *being*. Our Lord calls us to choose "the better part" by offering all our work in the home to him—being content with our duties in serving our family members and also seeking times to be at his feet in prayer and adoration. When we are unable to be at Our Lord's feet because we are busy *doing* for our family, we can be comforted knowing that Our Lord has placed us in our mothering role and considers our acts of love to our family as serving him too. When we give everything to Our Lord—a full surrender to him—we are choosing "the better part."

St. John of the Cross reminds us, "Contemplation is nothing else but a secret, peaceful and loving infusion of God, which, if admitted, will set the soul on fire with the Spirit of love." Let's see if we mothers can find Our Lord in the spirit of quiet during the present moments of our lives even during the busyness of our household activities and chores—in the midst of the pots and pans, diaper changes, and checking off "to-do" lists. He is there waiting to set our souls on fire!

SOMETHING TO PONDER

How can I possibly live in the present moment when I have so much on my mind and on my shoulders?

RECIPE FOR ENJOYING
THE GRACE OF THE PRESENT MOMENT

I will pray for the grace to live in the here and now.

I will trust God through prayer, and I will stop lamenting over my yesterdays and worrying about my tomorrows.

MOUNTAINS ARE MOVED

Sometimes it may seem that there is not a very lot
Noteworthy happening during the day at home.
Clothes are washed, meals are prepared,
The house is cleaned, stories are read, faces are washed,
Games are played, the children are guided,
Lessons are taught, prayers are said.
Yet a prayerful mother, by God's grace,
Being obedient to her state of life,
Listening to God's gentle promptings in her soul,
And offering her daily tasks to Our Lord, with love,
Can move mountains!
Our Lord will never fail to hear the prayers of a faithful mother.

*Dear Jesus, please continue to hear the prayers of mothers around the world
pleading for your help for their children.
Mary, Mother of Jesus, be Mother to me now
and please guide my mothering.*

HEART MOMENTS CANNOT BE TAKEN

While I am pulled
In many directions
To focus on issues and events,
Even essential ones,
I know that throughout these times
My heart will remain united to yours

And these heart moments
Cannot be taken by anyone or anything.
Thank you, Lord, for your amazing love!

Oh, Lord, please, join my heart to yours.
Help me to be like Martha and Mary at the same time!
Jesus, I trust in You.

— 27 —

RAISING SAINTS
TO HEAVEN

Not to go along the way to God is to go back. Perfect married life means the spiritual dedication of the parents for the benefit of their children.
—St. Thomas Aquinas

Life in a family is not always picture-perfect. There are squabbles and fights and maybe a few colorful metaphors expressed here and there, if you get my drift! Mothers are there to steady the ship, keep the peace, and correct the children—perhaps even at times keeping them from killing one another! Does this look like an illustration out of *Butler's Lives of the Saints*? You may be surprised to find out that many of the saints were mischievous little children at one time. We are not born with those sparkling halos I've been talking about, after all. At our baptisms we are purified, and our "halos" are brilliant. When we are a bit older and reach the age of reason (about seven years old) and are able to express our free will, that's when our halos can start to tarnish or even fall off! Not to worry, though, we are a work in progress, and the good Lord gives us umpteen chances in life to turn ourselves around and get with the program, so to speak. However, we shouldn't squander any opportunity to draw closer to God and to guide our children ever closer. Throughout life, we actually work out our salvation through give-and-take right within the walls of the domestic church so that we can finally earn a real halo when we reach our eternal reward!

Along with the unforgettable memory I expressed in an earlier chapter of kneeling down together with my siblings and my mother to pray the family Rosary is woven another recollection. I must confess that one time when we were praying together I did something a little out of character even for me at that time. I quietly sneaked a big and very plumy feather off the desk behind us where we were praying and used it to tickle the bottoms of my younger brother's bare feet as he knelt there praying. It was so tempting—seeing that fluffy feather on the desk just begging to be used for a tickle. I thought it would be fun. I was at times mischievous! Kids act like kids, and my mother was very patient with my shenanigans. I'm sorry, dear Lord and Blessed Mother Mary, that I interrupted our prayer time!

In getting our children headed in the right direction in life, we start with the sacrament of baptism, and from there we lead our children further down the narrow path that leads to heaven. The *Catechism* tells us,

Where infant baptism has become the form in which this sacrament is usually celebrated, it has become a single act encapsulating the preparatory stages of Christian initiation in a very abridged way. By its very nature infant baptism requires a *post-baptismal catechumenate*. Not only is there a need for instruction after baptism, but also for the necessary flowering of baptismal grace in personal growth. The *catechism* has its proper place here. (CCC, 1231)

It continues,

For all the baptized, children and adults, faith must grow *after* baptism. For this reason, the Church celebrates each year at the Easter Vigil the renewal of the baptismal promises. Preparation for baptism leads only to the threshold of new life. Baptism is the source of that new life in Christ from which the entire Christian life springs forth.

For the grace of baptism to unfold, the parents' help is important. So too is the role of the *godfather* and *godmother*, who must be firm believers, able and ready to help the newly baptized—the child or adult—on the road of Christian life. Their task is a truly ecclesial function (*officium*). The whole ecclesial community bears some responsibility for the development and safeguarding of the grace given at baptism. (CCC, 1254,1255)

Let's be sure to choose godparents for our children wisely. They play an important role in our children's lives. I am so happy and very fortunate to have Father John A. Hardon, SJ, as my daughter Mary-Catherine's godfather. I am sure that his prayers from heaven are guiding us now. Let's also be mindful of our responsibility as parents to continually provide instruction to our youngsters as our *Catechism* teaches, "for the necessary flowering of baptismal grace in personal growth." I very much like the image of *flowering* baptismal grace!

Raising our children every day becomes yet another teachable moment for us and for our families. We have been given the gift of raising little saints to heaven! Imagine that! Therefore, we can view our role in the family not as just going through the motions of our daily tasks but as truly making a tremendously significant impact on the lives of other human beings who have been entrusted to us. This entrusting is not something to be taken lightly. Our Lord has entrusted precious lives to us because he has faith in us to raise our children properly and bring them to him.

"The moral and spiritual strength of a woman is joined to her awareness that God *entrusts the human being to her in a special way.* Of course, God entrusts every human being to each and every other human being. But this entrusting concerns women in a special way—precisely by reason of their femininity—and this in a particular way determines their vocation" (*Mulieris Dignitatem*, 30).

We must be sure to teach the faith to our children, and if they receive additional religious instruction at school or from our parish, we must be sure that the courses are approved totally by the Church. There is a lot of mediocre and even bad teaching out there disguised as Church teaching. It may take a little time and effort to find what the best programs and courses are, but aren't your kids worth it? Aren't you also going to be held accountable before God? I would say that those two reasons should drive a parent toward seeking what is appropriate for their children.

While raising our children we should also strive to keep the communication lines open so that as issues pop up, we can handle them and discuss them with our children. We pray that we will live up to Our Lord's call to us to raise our little ones to him. He will give us all the necessary graces and strength to get through each day in our households, no matter what we are facing. Our recourse to prayer is our saving grace!

— 28 —
READY TO LEAVE
THE NEST

Our children are on loan to us to raise and help mold their consciences within the hearts of our homes, steering them to the straight and narrow path that leads to heaven. Of course, we most likely are not thinking about this *loan* from Our Lord when our infant child is lying against our heart sleeping away while sweet newborn baby smells and soft coos are permeating our world. One day we do have to give them back, though. I'm truly sorry to burst your bubble.

I felt those "giving back" pangs intensely each time our car pulled out of the driveway to take one of my children back to college for a new semester after their break, and I felt them when each of the older ones left the nest to start life on their own. It is with bittersweet emotion that we release our children so they can spread their wings. For me it is mostly bitter, not so much sweet, because I hate to see them go. Certainly, I do know in my heart that they need to embark upon life themselves and are no longer little children. But I really think that no amount of preparation can truly get a mother ready for these times. Besides, a mother is usually so immersed in the day-to-day moments of her life that time sneaks up on her, and she doesn't really have a chance to prepare herself for the fact that her offspring will indeed spring forth from the nest.

The good news is that they always return, and we will have many times to come together as a family and enjoy one another's company. I can never quite understand the parents who express that they can't wait for their children to embark upon their own lives and leave the nest! It's usually the same ones who said that they couldn't wait for their children to get their driver's license so they "don't have to cart them around anymore!" I am never in a rush to push them out before it's the right time.

I am reminded of the time when my daughter Jessica traveled to India with a few other college students to study there for a semester. A lump grew in my throat as I poured Jessica's cup of tea down the sink just after she left for the airport. As I stood at the kitchen sink for a moment, I stared out the window. *It would be the last cup of tea that I could make for her for more than four months,* I thought. She didn't even have time to drink it as she bustled around the house, gathering everything she would need for her trip to India—since she was too tired to pack the night before—checking off the two lists I had made for her of what needed to be done and what needed to be packed. Still, with all our plans and preparation, we are notorious for always running around at the last minute in a bit of a panic.

But, after all, it wasn't just *any* trip. It was a trip that would take my daughter very far away from us for a long period of time—a trip that required Jessica to prepare for ahead of time with notarized documents for power of attorney, many inoculations, prescriptions for medications, passport, visa, and plenty more details. She would need to take antimalarial medicine a few days before leaving, every day while she was in India, and for a couple of weeks after she arrived home.

I admired Jessica's courage, open mind, and energy to embark on such a trip as a college student abroad. However, my mother's heart was concerned about the travel and what lay ahead for her, being so far from home for so long in a foreign country—where disease may be rampant and foods, though perhaps enjoyable to her, may cause havoc to her small, delicate body. Will she get homesick? What if she gets sick? (She did get sick in Bangladesh. And then there was the monsoon in Bangladesh while she was there that took over one thousand lives; at the time, I had received no word from Jessica for days because the electrical power was out in many places.) All kinds of questions spun through my brain. But my mother's heart placed my daughter in Jesus's arms and under Mary's mantle. I enveloped her in prayer unceasingly, as did the rest of our family and friends. It's all I could do. I had to trust and let go.

That night when all was quiet, I sat on Jessica's bed to say some more prayers for her and her fellow group of students. I felt blessed and comforted to be able to pray from a special prayer book that belonged to my dear friend Father Bill. I didn't hold back on any prayers to our Blessed Mother and prayers for protection from the mighty archangels and the beloved saints. The next day I exhaled a big sigh of relief when I got word of my daughter's safe arrival in India—thank God.

One time my youngest daughter, Mary-Catherine, went into her brother Joseph's bedroom to feed his tortoise since Joseph was away at college. I had previously stripped Joseph's bed, planning to put fresh sheets on it before his return home. But I was not in any hurry to do so since Joseph would be away for a while, and I got busy with other things. When Mary-Catherine saw Joseph's bed looking so empty, she came out quickly and said to me, "Mom, can you please put some sheets on Joseph's bed—it looks so depressing!" She missed him, and so did I. We were not used to having him away. It was terrible!

To me, it just doesn't feel right after a child has left the nest. I don't like sitting down to dinner with that empty chair across the table from me reminding me of my child's absence. I am very proud of my son Joseph, who worked very hard at his studies and has been greatly involved in community service. *But why did he have to grow up so fast?* I wondered. The day we took him to his dorm at college and helped him get set up is a day I'll never forget. The entire two-hour car ride home I wore my sunglasses to hide the tears that continued to well up in my eyes. I was happy for Joseph to begin his college career, but my mother's heart was feeling a great loss. My little boy had grown up far too fast for my liking.

I've talked with a lot of parents who miss their kids when they leave home. One mom I know, Tina, told me that she thinks she needs some "serious counseling"! She doesn't like her son out of the house so much, embarking on his career after high school. She doesn't care for it at all, she admitted. Another mom, Diana, told me that she cried for a couple of weeks before her son left for college because he was the last one leaving the nest. She is trying to adjust and added that she is happy that he does call home frequently to ask her laundry questions.

One mom said, "This continual process of detachment from our children is an important part of growing in holiness for mothers in particular. I feel it the moment my child emerges from my womb. I become keenly aware that 'you' are not 'me.' Out of the cradle into the crib; big-boy pants; senior pictures; college visits; graduations: kindergarten, eighth grade, high school, college—each is a stab to the heart. 'You, my child, are becoming the person God wants you to be,' I remind myself. A sorrowful mother, I rejoice nonetheless. 'Unless a grain of wheat falls to the ground and dies, it will not have life.'"

Another seasoned mom who missed her kids once they were out of the nest told me, "My child leaving home for college is one of those developmental milestones that has helped me grow up too. Sometimes I have even pouted, like a scorned lover, when she doesn't call some night. Now I'm almost relieved if I don't receive several calls a day: it means she's happy! She's becoming a young woman, not remaining a specimen held in captivity by her mother. I know that our love for our children is greater than our pain, which is probably driven by fear of loss and selfishness. Truly saints are born of—and raised by—holy parents."

One parent explained, "My older son left for the service right after high school, just in time for the first Gulf War. The glaring emptiness was made more difficult by the daily realization that it might be permanent."

Every parent feels the pangs and goes through growth, too, when their children grow up before their eyes—one day to leave the nest. When my son Joseph left for college, I likened the feeling I had to that of a mother bird pushing her baby bird out of the nest, but I didn't feel quite ready to give that last push. There are parents who can't wait for the "freedom" they anticipate they will enjoy when their children leave home, thinking that they've raised them for many years and now they want to relax or travel. While I personally don't understand that kind of thinking, I do realize that not every parent can relate to the "empty hole" feeling I have when my children leave.

One year, it was doubly hard for me because I also missed my daughter Jessica who went back to college a few days after Joseph left. Jessica attends a college out of state. Yet I was so proud of her too. She worked very hard and excelled at college. She also has a big heart and has done a lot of community-service volunteering.

A mom recently got in touch with me who also experienced that "big hole" feeling that I described regarding our kids being absent from the home. She said, "I'm finding unexpected holes in the fabric of our family life, right alongside the ones I've expected. Who knew it would hurt so much, feel so strange? I am holding fast to the hope that there are unexpected joys soon to come as well."

I told her, "There will be unexpected blessings and joys (I know, because Joseph is my fourth child to 'leave the nest'). But for now, we have that big hole in our family's tapestry. It's tough to push our children forth, but we do it with God's blessings and continued prayers. Don't worry, they'll be back!"

One such blessing I'll tell you about now. One time, several years ago, my daughter Chaldea came over for dinner. She was embarking on a trip across the country that day. (*Oh my*, I thought, *lots of Rosaries are in order here!*) She came over to spend some time before leaving for her two-week trip. We had dinner together, and then I took out the big brown bag of apples I had bought earlier so I could make apple crisp for dessert. Chaldea and I sat at the kitchen table, conversing and peeling that big mound of apples. Mary-Catherine had lots of homework that night; otherwise she would have been right there helping with the apple peeling.

What a treat it was for me to have uninterrupted time with my daughter as we peeled the apples and chatted. I put the rest of the ingredients together for three pans of apple crisp, and Chaldea popped onto the Internet on a laptop in the kitchen to show me the places where she would be visiting. We find these blessings of times together with our grown children woven throughout our lives while we live in the present moments—thanking God for his love for us!

I remember how hard it was for me when Chaldea left the nest—ushering another "child" into adulthood. I am so very proud of her for all her accomplishments, but mostly for her kind and loving heart! She is a treasure, to be sure. I cherished our moments making apple crisp together that night. *Something she may not realize or fully understand*, I thought, *until she has her own children*. But I think she knows how happy I am to be with her and with all my children. Now, at the writing of this book, my daughter Chaldea is mother to a two-year-old son and a brand-new baby, Leo Arthur (my two grandsons who light up my life!).

Before Chaldea left the nest, it was the turn of my oldest, Justin. Justin probably had the hardest time leaving home because none of his siblings would allow it! When he was in his early twenties, he discussed with the family the possibility of his moving out. As much as I knew that the fateful dreaded day would finally arrive, I couldn't bear to think about it; it was too upsetting—my first "baby" to leave. Well, Justin's baby sister, Mary-Catherine, saved the day and did not make it easy for him at all! She wrote him a big note, scribbled in her best handwriting, and taped it to his bedroom door:

"Justin, DON'T LEAVE!" So he didn't leave! How could he? Three powerful, simple, and succinct words changed my firstborn's mind. Actually, it was the love behind those words. I sense that he felt the love and knew we weren't ready to let him go. Finally, a year or more later, it was time for Justin to launch out on his own.

I know many a Christian mother who imitates St. Monica's unceasing prayers for her child, Augustine. A mother's job is never complete. Just because her child has left the nest does not mean that she is finished with mothering her "child." While the young adult navigates life on his or her own, there will be times when the "child" needs reassurance, guidance, or some sort of help. A mother chooses wisely and prays to discern when she should step forward to offer advice and when she should not. She learns the dance. She, of course, is delighted when her "child" comes to her for her guidance and counsel. No matter what, a faithful mother's prayers will never cease for her grown children. That would surely be impossible. When the cord was cut at her child's birth, the mother still remained totally connected with her baby. When the front door shuts and that grown child walks down the front walk to the new life ahead of him or her, a mother is still very connected. She will always be connected with her "babies" spiritually throughout eternity. A mother's prayers are powerful. A mother's love never stops.

To all the parents out there with very young children, you may think that this talk about college and kids leaving the nest certainly could not possibly pertain to your life. After all, there is your little darling in your arms or on your lap. Trust me, please—they grow quickly, and I haven't found a way to slow down time yet. Time marches on, and we don't have the ability to slow it down or stop it. Enjoy your family life, hanging on to your dinners together and your times together. Later on, down the road, that little baby that you are holding in your arms now will be all grown up and will bring back his or her own children to visit you—or possibly he will be behind the altar saying Mass or she will be in the convent! Who knows?

In response to that mom I mentioned earlier who was wondering about "unexpected blessings and joys" after the children have left home, I say, *Yes!* The blessings will come—they are found in our everyday lives. We have to seek them when we can, grab onto them, and cherish them! The holes will be filled up with the tremendous blessing of seeing our children blossom into adults with grace, and then we can welcome them back with big hugs and kisses each time they step back over the threshold and into our domestic churches once again. By God's good grace, throughout our vocation of motherhood, we will raise all our little saints to heaven!

SOMETHING TO PONDER

How can I teach my children the path of holiness when they seem to be anything but saintlike right now?

RECIPE: A LITTLE LEAVEN—
RAISING SAINTS TO HEAVEN

Patience is the ingredient that allows me to realize that my family is a true work in progress. My children's halos may become tarnished or even fall off at times, but I have to put one foot in front of the other each day, always setting the example for my children and always teaching them. I will keep walking in faith, and I will continue to pray.

RAISING UP SOLDIERS FOR CHRIST
Little precious souls entrusted to our care,
Each one so very different from the other,
Needing to be loved and nurtured individually
And taught about God and life.
By our love, example, and diligent teaching,
Our children, having had a strong beginning and foundation,
Will grow up steadfast in their faith,
Serving Our Lord in gratitude and love,
Soldiers for Christ,
And one day will return to him.

Dear Blessed Mother Mary, teach me to be content with
my vocation as a mother.
Help me to guide my children in holiness.

— 29 —

DISCOVERING GRACE WITHIN SUFFERING

"My God, I choose everything. I will not be a saint by halves. I am not afraid of suffering for thee."
—St. Thérèse of Lisieux

Motherhood is not typically viewed as a role of suffering. It is a vocation overflowing with deep joy, hugs, and giggles, after all. We would, of course, be fooling ourselves or living in a fantasy world if we didn't admit that there is some amount of sacrifice involved in rearing our children. I don't think we'll have any arguing there. St. Teresa of Calcutta didn't mince words when she told us, "To love properly there must be sacrifice."

Delving deeper than the outward appearances, we discover that intertwined with the "warm fuzzies" derived from newborn baby smells, dimpled elbows, and soft coos— as well as the warm embraces from the chubby little arms of our toddlers and the feelings of satisfaction from watching our older children achieve their goals—there is a certain amount of suffering that goes with the territory. Motherhood, after all, is a tapestry of joy and suffering woven together as one beautiful work of art.

St. John Paul II tells us, "Humanity's future depends on people who rely on the truth and whose lives are enlightened by lofty moral principles that enable their hearts to love to the point of sacrifice." This is what a mother's life is precisely all about—loving to the point of sacrifice. Unless you are a mother, it may be too difficult to comprehend the necessity for sacrifice and perhaps also the ability to embrace a life spattered with sacrifice.

Not every mother desires to embrace a lifestyle in which she is being asked—on a regular basis, I might add—to give until it hurts. This whole concept of giving and hurting may seem absurd, especially in today's culture. Why should we feel uncomfortable—God forbid—or *selfless*, when we can avoid it? It's because the love in our motherly hearts calls us to it; it beckons us to give of ourselves unreservedly. Real love demands blood, sweat, and tears. If we run from the sacrifice and suffering, we are abandoning our responsibility to our children and families, and we are also turning our backs on God. Our world clamors for us to embrace comfort, while Our Lord lovingly and consistently calls us to sacrifice for the love of our families. Which call will we answer?

Mother Teresa reminded us, "A living love hurts. Jesus to prove his love for us, died on the Cross. The mother to give life to her child has to suffer. If you really love one another properly, there must be sacrifice." However, to some, this notion may seem paradoxical or even ludicrous. In his apostolic letter *Novo Millennio Ineunte*, St. John Paul II explained that the faithful are called to experience "the paradoxical blending of bliss and pain" when following Our Lord Jesus (27).

Earlier, I quoted St. Therese: "My God, I choose everything. I will not be a saint by halves. I am not afraid of suffering for thee." Are we courageous and bold enough to want and ask for *everything*—the bliss *and* the pain— both together? In doing so, we will be able to experience motherhood in its deeply intrinsically holy and very beautiful manner.

— 30 —

OPPORTUNITIES FOR GRACE

God is our refuge and strength,
a very present help in trouble.
Therefore we will not fear.
—Psalm 46:1–2

We learn from the *Catechism* and the Bible: "The way of perfection passes by way of the Cross. There is no holiness without renunciation and spiritual battle. Spiritual progress entails the ascesis and mortifications that gradually lead to living in the peace and joy of the Beatitudes" (CCC, 2015).

Suffering may not be necessarily what we want to embrace or even desire a little bit. However, suffering is not avoidable in anyone's life. As we progress in holiness, putting one foot in front of the other in our domestic churches, ministering to our families, Our Lord will indeed give us many opportunities to earn graces through the suffering and sacrifice. We begin to see and experience further the intricate tapestry of motherhood—a blending of "bliss and pain." In time, we will be able to tell Our Lord that we truly want what he wants, period. Our Lord will lead us toward him through our joys and our sorrows. He'll give us strength every step of the way even when we can't feel it—he is with us always.

In *Deus Caritas Est*, Pope Emeritus Benedict XVI has assured us that God is always present even when he seems to be absent because of his silence at a particular time of our lives. Pope Benedict XVI said, "Often our deepest cause of suffering is the very absence of God (31)." It is then when we must pray for an increased faith. We will then know that he is purifying our souls of hindrances and burnishing them to allow for a closer union with him.

Father John Hardon, SJ, defined suffering this way: "The disagreeable experience of soul that comes with the presence of evil or the privation of some good." Father Hardon explained that even though we commonly associate suffering with pain, suffering is more accurately "the reaction to pain, and in this sense suffering is a decisive factor in Christian spirituality." He added that "suffering is the result of sin having entered the world. Its purpose, however, is not only to expiate wrongdoing, but to enable the believer to offer God a sacrifice of praise of his divine right over creatures." He further explained that through prayer we are to unite ourselves with Christ in his sufferings "as an expression of love, and in the process to become more like Christ, who, having joy set before him, chose the Cross, and thus 'to make up all that has still to be undergone by Christ for the sake of His body, the Church' (Col 1:24)."

Graces are merited through struggles and sacrifice, and this is where sanctification occurs. Many of the saints took extra suffering upon themselves because they were divinely inspired to do so to grow in holiness and to overcome a sinful nature. Some saints wore a hair shirt, which was an undergarment woven with very itchy animal hair that then lay against the bare skin to act as a constant, itchy aggravation. Can you imagine wearing a hair shirt? I would want to rip it off in a matter of minutes. Some other saints used other means to inflict some sort of suffering to their flesh, such as chains around the waist or ankles, or choosing to sleep on hard wooden beds without mattresses. Numerous saints practiced various forms of mortifications, or "self-discipline," to bring on discomfort or pain. Mortifications were a practice of Christian asceticism designed for the purpose of doing penance or to master one's sinful tendencies. The saints desired to grow in virtue and to become more like Jesus.

By utilizing supernatural mortifications, based on faith and cooperating with God's grace, a person will grow in holiness. Our lives are filled with countless opportunities for mortification and sacrifice so that we too can grow in holiness. Let's not forget that we are all called to sanctity. Sanctity is not just reserved for the saints! So, while a typical Christian mother most likely will not be wearing a hair shirt, she may find other opportunities to "wear" a hair shirt. For instance, a family member or neighbor can bring about the same type of annoying or aggravating "itchiness." In order to merit graces and grow in holiness, we can respond appropriately with what is pleasing to God rather than to snap back at the rude comment or criticism that was aimed at us or sulk because of the situation. Instead, we can choose the high road, "bite our tongue," and respond in love. Therefore, people and things around us that can cause us discomfort, or that will challenge us in some way, can become our "hair shirts." Keeping our lips sealed (in certain circumstances, because sometimes it is appropriate to speak up charitably to right a wrong, for instance) then becomes an excellent chance for earning grace. How many times do we blurt out a remark or comment, only moments later wishing we had not? We earn graces for ourselves and others when we master our bad habits, with God's help.

Another type of mortification that we can exercise in order to merit graces for ourselves or others is to do without luxuries at times, which is very similar to fasting or abstaining from certain foods. If there is something you would really enjoy and may actually crave, stop for a moment and make a decision to do without it for the sake of a grace you hope to receive or graces for your husband or children. Perhaps you are looking forward to a hot bath or a long, hot shower. You can choose to do without the luxurious bath or cut the time down on your shower and offer the little sacrifice to Our Lord with love—asking him to grant you the grace you need for yourself and your family. Any little or big sacrifice offered with love to the Father will be blessed. Some may view this way of thinking as absolutely crazy, especially since this is not the way of the world. We are not of the world, though, right? Additionally, you won't be shouting from the rooftops that you are performing these efforts of mortifications and penances; rather, you pray quietly, do your sacrifices, and offer them all to Our Lord in secret. No one should know about them except for your spiritual director and Our Lord.

Inevitably, there are certain times when all our good plans and intentions are turned on end. We may have put aside a quiet time for meditation and prayer or planned a chunk of time to finally tackle a project with its deadline looming over us. Suddenly, our plans are rearranged by a sick child or a household situation that needs to be addressed immediately. What will my response be? Pouting or fuming? Questioning? Or surrendering to God and the fact that he is in control? We can offer up the feelings of the pangs of sacrifice to Our Lord so that he can transform them into graces for our families.

At other times, a mother's sacrifice might require putting her own desires aside for a while in order to raise her children properly with her full attention, as I have mentioned before. An abundance of material things is not necessary—an abundance of love, time, and devotion is. A faithful mother gives up what she might have been able to achieve or acquire so that she may answer Our Lord with her wholehearted "yes" to life and "yes" to all it entails.

There are many single and faithful Christian mothers living in our midst. I used to be among them. Many single mothers live with many kinds of suffering. Sometimes because of their situation, they may be living without many luxuries, and they may have barely enough money to survive, particularly as they strive to be present to their children and raise them properly. They may not have relatives nearby to help either. They could also feel lonely in a couple's world. Yet, through their day-to-day sacrifices, they put one foot in front of the other each day to bring their children ever closer to God.

St. Francis de Sales told us, "The state of marriage is one that requires more virtue and constancy than any other. It is a perpetual exercise in mortification." Let's ponder that statement for a few moments at least! Other instances where we may grow in holiness and merit graces occur when we surrender our lives over to Our Lord and accept whatever he gives us. Whether we live in a castle or a shack, we can thank Our Lord for his love and blessings. At times, we may feel annoyed because certain household projects or renovations remain unfinished due to lack of time, money, or both. We can offer our feelings of frustration to God and accept our circumstances. Our husbands may be extra busy at work, and we miss them as much as the children do. Here's where our 150/150 percent marital partnership that I recommend comes in. There are times when we are required to give more of ourselves for the sake of our spouse and the family. We give, and we accept. This too shall pass. It's a very good thing that our husbands are employed, when we know that there are others who are not. Let's not complain; instead, let's be supportive of our husbands, who are doing their best to provide for our families.

Charles de Foucauld has said,

> In this sad world, there is a joy at the heart of things which is not shared by either the saints in heaven or the angels—that of suffering with our beloved. However hard life may be, however long our days of sadness may endure . . . we must never seek to leave the foot of the cross sooner than God would have us do . . . our master having been good enough to let us experience, if not always its sweetness, then at least its beauty and necessity for those who love it.

Our Lord knows what we need and when we need it. We must trust him as our divine physician. Charles de Foucauld explains the necessity in our suffering at the foot of the cross as well as its sweetness. It is a sweetness that will be understood as we surrender our lives over to Our Lord. He wants all our hearts—every piece—in full surrender.

And if we need some uplifting words of encouragement to help us through our suffering, we can think about what St. John of the Cross has said: "The soul of one who loves God always swims in joy, always keeps holiday, and is always in the mood for singing." Isn't that nice? Are we singing? Perhaps maybe after we practice what St. Thomas Aquinas has recommended, we will sing! He said, "Sorrow can be alleviated by good sleep, a bath, and a glass of wine." Now here's a man after my own heart! However, I must confess that because my life is so busy at this moment, I rarely do get enough good sleep (I try) or have the luxury of a bath (I take a quick shower instead). But a glass of wine once in a while sounds like a splendid idea! I know that St. John of the Cross's advice is very good food for the soul indeed. We can also find much comfort in St. Ignatius Loyola's wise words: "If God causes you to suffer much, it is a sign that he has great designs for you, and that he certainly intends to make you a saint."

I am reminded of a seminarian who put very little food on his plate for lunch. Mother Teresa entered the dining room for a short visit with the seminarians. She noticed the young man's sparse plate of food. In a sort of dramatic motion, she lifted a huge serving platter and scraped a lot of food on the seminarian's plate. She leaned in and said, "You won't be able to take care of the needs of the poor very well if you have a hungry belly." She was a wise woman indeed. Let's be sure to find a proper balance with our mortifications and fasting, not overdoing it. Mothers need to take care of themselves so they can care for others, as Mother Teresa suggested to the seminarian.

SOMETHING TO PONDER

Why should I desire to embrace suffering in my role as mother?

RECIPE FOR DELICIOUS DISCOVERIES:
FINDING GRACE WITHIN SUFFERING

When I'm suffering, I will remember that according to St. Teresa of Calcutta, "To love properly, there must be sacrifice." I will ask God for strength and grace to endure my suffering, as well as offer it to God and ask him to use it to help my soul and to aid others.

SEEN BY GOD ALONE

Her hands are red, wrinkled, and chapped from the bitter wind
As she pins the clothespins, one after another,
To the line of clothes, already stiffening in the freezing temperature.
The bitter wind mercilessly lifts at the hem of her coat,
Attempting to blow through her clothes and whip at her back.
She briskly continues her loving tasks,
Unnoticed by the speeding motorists passing by.
Only Our Lord sees her putting out her family's laundry to dry,
Stretching out her arms,
Hanging out one wet article of clothing after another,
As only a mother's love can.
Our Lord will never fail to notice all mothers'
Seemingly hidden loving acts of service to their families
All around the world.

Jesus, Mary, and Joseph, have mercy on us and pray for us.
Jesus, I trust in you!

BRING MY HEART TO YOURS

You know, Lord, how I long to kneel before you
In the Blessed Sacrament,
Where you reside in the tabernacle,
Waiting for visitors to come and be with you.
But you have put me here
In the midst of my family.
At times, I feel there are just not enough hours in the day
And here I am trying to catch up
With the never-ending chores of motherhood.
Please, Lord, bring my heart to yours
Where it can drink in your grace and peace
And rest before you for a while.
My heart will embrace yours.
Please accept this prayer from my heart:
I pray that you will remain with me
Throughout all my days,
To give me the strength and grace that I so need as a mother.
Thank you, dear Lord, for your love!

*Most Sacred Heart of Jesus, have mercy on us. Immaculate Heart of
Mary, pray for us.*

SAINTLY INSPIRATION

All Christians in any state, or walk of life are called to the fullness of Christian life and to the perfection of charity.
—*Lumen Gentium,* 40, 2

Many of the saints can offer us inspiration and even intercession throughout our mothering days. By intercession, I mean that the saints actually pray for us! I am particularly fond of St. Teresa of Calcutta because in God's divine providence, I met this amazing woman and knew her for about ten years. I like to pass along the blessings and lessons of love that I have learned from her to others so that they will be blessed too! I don't wish to keep it all to myself. I always weave Mother Teresa's wisdom throughout my writings.

The saints were ordinary pilgrims like you and me who decided to follow Our Lord's beckoning. They responded to grace. They wanted to become holy by following in Our Lord's footsteps, guided by his great love, continual grace, and the Holy Spirit. Though they lived in many eras, their timeless wisdom and examples of great virtue can be an inspiration to sustain our hope and drive us forward in faith throughout our daily lives.

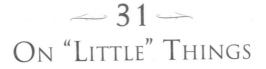

— 31 —
On "Little" Things

*Be faithful in small things because it is in
them that your strength lies.*
—St. Teresa of Calcutta

Mother Teresa had a great love for St. Thérèse of Lisieux,
who was sometimes called the "Little Flower" and "St. Thérèse
of the Child Jesus." Mother Teresa chose St. Thérèse's name
when she became a nun. Since the name *Therese* had been
taken by another nun, Mother Teresa chose the Spanish
version, "Teresa." She modeled herself after St. Thérèse and
often spoke about the "little way" of doing things—of being
attentive to the little details—and told us to do little things
with great love. St. Teresa of Calcutta has said, "So let us keep
very small and follow the Little Flower's way of trust, love,
and joy, and we will fulfill Mother's promise to give saints
to Mother Church." Through the enormity of her work, she
remained "small." Her smallness and great humility were the
secrets to her sanctity.

St. Thérèse prayed that all her actions would be
transformed into acts of love. She lived with a spirit of great

obedience, obeying her superiors—considering them to be God's representatives—and then trusting every situation to God, no matter what the outcome. She is most known for her "little way" because she humbly believed that even the smallest act of service to another could be a huge act of love that would transform the hearts and the souls for whom she prayed.

Regarding the importance of simplicity, one time St. Thérèse explained a passage that she was struck by in the Song of Songs to her fellow Carmelite nun, Marie of the Trinity. Regarding the part when the spouse says to the beloved, "We shall make chains of gold, inlaid with silver" (1:10), St. Thérèse said, "What a strange thing for the spouse to say!" She continued, "You would expect a silver chain inlaid with gold, or a gold chain inlaid with something more precious than itself. But Jesus has given me the key to the mystery: He has shown me that the gold chains are love, charity, but that he does not like them unless they are inlaid with the silver of childlike simplicity. God must value simplicity very highly to say He finds it fit to enhance the splendor of charity."

When St. Thérèse was unable to receive her Lord Jesus in Holy Communion, she deeply lamented. She sorely missed him in her heart and soul, so to remedy this situation she asked Our Lord to always remain in her heart. She said, "I know, my God, that when you want to give us more, you increase our desires. My heart is full of immense desires, and I confidently invite you to come and take possession of it. I cannot receive Holy Communion as often as I would like to,

Lord, but are you not all-powerful? Stay in me as you do in the tabernacle, and never leave this little host of yours."

Mother Teresa told the story about an elderly blind man she met in Australia who lived on a reservation among the Aborigines. She said that this poor man had been completely ignored by everyone, and his little home was filthy and very cluttered. He was unable to care for his home. Mother Teresa asked him if she could come by to clean his house and wash his clothes. He refused, explaining that he felt fine just the way he was living. Mother Teresa lovingly persisted until the man agreed. In cleaning his home, this humble nun discovered a very beautiful lamp that was covered with a thick layer of dust and cobwebs. She cleaned it off and asked the man why he didn't use it. He explained that there was no reason to use it because he never had visitors. Mother Teresa then asked him if he would light the lamp if the sisters came to see him. He replied, "Of course!"

Needless to say, the Missionaries of Charity sisters made a commitment to visit this man every evening from that day forward. They knew that they would be serving the man who was in need of companionship and also Jesus in that man because they firmly believed that what we do to each other, we do to Jesus (Matt. 25:31–46). A couple of years later, the Missionaries of Charity received a note from the man. He said, "Tell my friend that the light she lit in my life continues to shine still." Mother Teresa said she had forgotten all about that man and the light until she received his note.

By recounting the story of the man and the lamp, she wasn't attempting to say, "Look at the wonderful thing I have done for that man"; rather, I feel that she meant, "Look how meaningful and transforming a little thing can be for someone, especially when done with great love." We can apply this sentiment to our daily lives in the care of our family. There are so many things that we do in the course of our daily mothering that we couldn't possibly remember every single act of love. However, we should know that Our Lord sees every one and every one brings about transformation in one way or another.

Another time Mother Teresa's sisters came upon a man in Rome who had no contact with society at all. A mute, he stayed locked up in his little apartment. The sisters began to clean his apartment and wash his clothes regularly. Knowing the sisters, I can just imagine their joy and smiles as they bustled about his home, most likely singing or humming as they worked. The man said nothing. The sisters prepared food for him, too, and decided to visit him twice a day rather than only once a day since he was so secluded from humankind. After a few days, the sisters were surprised to hear this man speak. He said, "Sisters, you have brought God into my life. Bring me also a priest." After sixty years away from the Church, that man made his confession when the priest arrived to see him. He died the next day.

The sisters had carried God in their hearts to the man. In serving him with love and tenderness, they were able, by God's grace, to work an amazing miracle in his life by bringing him into the arms of Jesus before he left this planet. Doing little things with great love is the foundation of our daily lives as mothers too. We may never realize the amazing work that Our Lord is doing through us when we allow him to. We need to trust and believe.

In instructing her sisters about the holiness found in ordinary daily duties, St. Teresa of Calcutta has said,

Let us all become a true and fruitful branch on the vine Jesus, by accepting him in our lives as it pleases him to come: as the Truth, to be told; as the Life, to be lived; as the Light, to be lighted; as the Love, to be loved; as the way, to be walked; as the joy, to be given; as the Peace to be spread; as the sacrifice, to be offered, in our families and our neighbors.

What can we mothers learn from St. Thérèse and Mother Teresa? I think quite a bit!

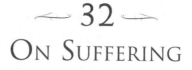

— 32 —
ON SUFFERING

St. Rose of Lima has said, "Without the burden of afflictions it is impossible to reach the height of grace. The gifts of grace increase as the struggles increase." Interesting words to ponder as we put one foot in front of the other each day in our households! St. Thérèse of Lisieux expressed in one of her poems, "Here on earth, to live for love does not mean settling on Thabor; it means climbing Calvary with Jesus and looking on the Cross as a treasure."

We can also learn much about suffering and "offering it up" to God from St. Thérèse. One day she expressed to a fellow nun how she felt about suffering before she became a nun. She said,

Before I entered, when I woke up in the morning I used to think about what the day might have in store for me, and if I foresaw annoying things I got up depressed. Now it's the opposite: the more opportunities I can foresee of bearing witness to my love for Jesus and of earning a living for my children [her children were the souls she prayed for], the poor sinners, the more joyful and courageous I am when I get up in the morning. The first thing I do is to kiss my crucifix. I then place it on my pillow while I dress, and I tell Jesus: "Look, you worked and wept enough for thirty-three years here on earth; today you can take a rest, it's my turn to fight and suffer."

Isn't that the sweetest sentiment, to tell Jesus he can take a rest?

St. Bernadette, who we know was privileged with the wondrous visions of the Blessed Mother at Lourdes, France, also endured much suffering and scorn later on from fellow nuns and superiors when she became a nun. Nevertheless, she had a heart full of compassion for those who suffered and prayed earnestly for them all. She encouraged and consoled the nuns around her who were in need of kind words and help. This was all during the time when she herself was treated harshly by her novice mistress and superiors even while she endured suffering from a tumor of the knee, attacks of asthma, lung hemorrhages, earaches, headaches, and later tuberculosis. Through the depths of her misery and pain, St. Bernadette remained humble, faithful, and loving. Our Lord was allowing her to suffer for him, and St. Bernadette's faithful heart didn't waste a minute of it; rather, she asked that it could be used for God's will, never expecting consolations in this life on earth.

St. Clare of Assisi gives us an interesting thought to ponder. She said, "Melancholy is the poison of devotion. When one is in tribulation, it is necessary to be more happy and more joyful because one is nearer to God." St. Clare's dear friend St. Francis of Assisi said, "Let the brothers ever avoid appearing gloomy, sad, and clouded, like the hypocrites; but let one ever be found joyous in the Lord, gay, amiable, gracious, as is meet." St. Clare also helps us with bearing our sacrifices and sufferings. She said, "Our labor here is brief, but the reward is eternal. Do not be disturbed by the clamor of the world which passes like a shadow. Do not let the false delights of a deceptive world deceive you." St. Clare's words are so very relevant to us mothers today.

St. Teresa of Avila, a doctor of the Church and someone who we know did not mince words—and who even questioned God's ways of dealing with her at times—said, "The sufferings God inflicts on contemplatives are so unbearable a kind, that, unless he sustained such souls with the manna of divine consolations, they would find their agony unbearable." St. Teresa of Calcutta told me that she felt that Jesus had allowed me to come so close to him on the Cross so that "he could kiss" me! I wrote about this in great detail in my spiritual memoir, *The Kiss of Jesus* (Ignatius Press, 2015). I had shared many personal things with this dear friend and spiritual advisor. I'll never forget her words to me. What does one say to words like that? I was speechless and humbled, and I felt a deep and perhaps undeserved joy and peace in my heart. When we are suffering deeply, we can be comforted knowing that Our Lord knows our sorrows and our pains and is closer to us than we can imagine!

── 33 ──
GO TO ST. JOSEPH

I'd like to share a few stories here about good St. Joseph and how he came to assist me, as well as my friends, in times of suffering. My dear friend and spiritual director, Father William C. Smith (whom I call Father Bill), told me long ago to "go to St. Joseph." He explained that since St. Joseph was the head of the Holy Family and helped and protected them, he would also help us in our family situations when we earnestly and faithfully called upon him. To this day, I have a very strong fondness for this great saint and a strong devotion to him. He has helped me out of many very difficult situations. I have recommended him to others, and they have also been helped by his intercession.

A friend of mine had asked for prayers because she was experiencing serious problems. Her adult son was addicted to cocaine. He was refusing to stay in the rehabilitation center and had become suicidal. Needless to say, this poor mother was suffering terribly out of love for her son and was desperate for help and prayers. Her pain and anguish were very deep. I recommended that this woman turn to St. Joseph. This mother and others in her prayer group invoked St. Joseph through a novena that ended exactly on St. Joseph's feast day.

Before too long I received word that the novena prayers to St. Joseph were answered! Her son experienced a major breakthrough and accepted help right on St. Joseph's feast day. St. Joseph had come through once again! A seemingly insurmountable situation had been taken care of by this awesome saint!

One day I had been discussing St. Joseph with a group of Catholic writers, and my friend Carrie agreed with my sentiments and chimed in and expressed her trust in St. Joseph and in his novena. She told us how he had helped her family in an extraordinary way. She said, "I also trust that the novena will move mountains. Turning to St. Joseph has always brought amazing results for me." She explained, "After I was told that I couldn't conceive post-chemotherapy, then getting pregnant and losing every baby at three months, my husband's heart was broken. I sent him to a local parish to sit beside a statue of St. Joseph, helping him to focus his prayers with those of the patron saint of fathers." Her husband prayed before the statue of the illustrious St. Joseph. Carrie continued, "Within days, I found out I was pregnant. Matteo Joseph was due on March 19 (St. Joseph's feast day), but arrived early. My daughter, Francesca Maria, was born two years later, on March 19." With great emotion, she expressed, "Not a soul on this planet can tell me that St. Joseph did not intercede on my behalf."

My friend added, "Joseph was truly holy. After all, he's the only person who ever lived with two people who never sinned! If something went wrong at home . . . well, you knew whose fault it was. No wonder Joseph is never quoted in the Bible," she quipped. "I too would probably keep my mouth shut under those circumstances. I've shared this story in the simple hope that you will find peace in these prayers."

My friend Sarah expressed her feelings about St. Joseph on her blog. She wrote,

> I never paid much attention to St. Joseph, aside from acknowledging him as the head of the Holy Family in a rather passing way. I never thought much about him, aside from his patronage of my lovely little parish. I really never asked for his intercession or pondered his special role in salvation history. It sounds silly to me now, but it just never occurred to me.
>
> Earlier this year, a friend—Donna-Marie—casually suggested (in a reply to a long, whining, "my-husband's-job-stinks-blah-blah-blah" email from me) that we pray a St. Joseph novena together. It was like a slap to the forehead, and it wasn't from the friend who's usually my novena buddy.
>
> A novena to St. Joseph made sense in so many ways— he's the patron of fathers and workers, not to mention families. Wouldn't he have a special interest in my little family? And couldn't his prayers, perhaps, be especially close to God, seeing as how God trusted Joseph with his Son and all?

So we started our novena. A few days into it, my husband got a call asking him if he would be interested in an interview with a company that he had just sent a resume to. The day after his interview, our second daughter was born. On the last day of the novena, he received a call asking him to come in for a second interview. Needless to say, I started a second novena of thanksgiving.

I personally can't thank St. Joseph enough for his great care for my own family. As I mentioned earlier, many years ago, my spiritual director and dear friend Father Bill introduced me to St. Joseph. One time I was having some trouble with some neighbors who were very unruly. I was a single mother at the time, living in a two-family house. The upstairs neighbors were usually drunk and even dropped bowling balls on their floor (my ceiling) to disturb me! I'm serious—I know this may be hard to believe, but they actually did! Almost every weekend, the man who lived upstairs with his girlfriend would come home very late and very drunk, and he would start pounding on my walls, yelling the most obscene and terrible threatening things I have ever heard. I had to call the police each time, and I really feared for my safety and that of my children. The police came out each time, but the man never got into much trouble until one time when they caught him in action. Then, of course, I had to be concerned that this man was going to retaliate because I had called the police on him each time.

My dear Father Bill told me that I did the right thing, of course, by calling the police. My brother decided to move in with me temporarily to be sure that I was safe. Father Bill also encouraged me to call upon St. Joseph and again explained to me that since he was the head of the Holy Family, he would help my family too. I began a thirty-day novena that very day. On the thirtieth day, I heard the sound of a big truck outside. I looked out my window and could not believe my eyes! There was a moving truck out front, and I saw that the upstairs neighbors were moving out! What an answer to prayer! I knew that St. Joseph had intervened and helped us.

St. Joseph continued to help us on more occasions than I can possibly tell you. I have "introduced" him to many people because I know that his intercession is very powerful and he is a loving father. I know that he has helped in so many ways. St. Teresa of Avila said that he never failed to help her.

I have probably passed out thousands of prayer cards of St. Joseph and the thirty-day novena prayers to him. Years ago I owned and operated a Catholic book and religious articles store. I named it "St. Joseph's Corner"! I also named one of my sons Joseph after dear St. Joseph.

This is the prayer I prayed when I was in the situation with the not-so-nice neighbors and for all other help within our family:

THIRTY-DAY NOVENA TO SAINT JOSEPH
in honor of the years he spent with Jesus and Mary, for any
special intention.

*Ever blessed and glorious Joseph, kind and loving father,
and helpful friend of all in sorrow! You are the good father and
protector of orphans, the defender of the defenseless, the patron of
those in need and sorrow. Look kindly on my request. My sins
have drawn down on me the just displeasure of my God, and so I
am surrounded with unhappiness. To you, loving guardian of the
Family of Nazareth, do I go for help and protection.*

*Listen, then, I beg you, with fatherly concern, to my earnest
prayers, and obtain for me the favors I ask.*

*I ask it by the infinite mercy of the eternal Son of God, which
moved him to take our nature and to be born into this world of
sorrow.*

*I ask it by the weariness and suffering you endured when you
found no shelter at the inn of Bethlehem for the holy Virgin, nor a
place where the Son of God could be born. Then, being everywhere
refused, you had to allow the Queen of Heaven to give birth to the
world's Redeemer in a cave.*

*I ask it by the loveliness and power of that sacred name,
Jesus, which you conferred on the adorable Infant.*

*I ask it by that painful torture you felt at the prophecy
of Simeon, which declared the Child Jesus and his Holy Mother
future victims of our sins and of their great love for us.*

*I ask it through your sorrow and pain of soul when the
angel declared to you that the life of the Child Jesus was sought by*

his enemies. From their evil plan you had to flee with him and his Blessed Mother into Egypt. I ask it by all the suffering, weariness, and labors of that long and dangerous journey.

I ask it by all your care to protect the Sacred Child and his Immaculate Mother during your second journey, when you were ordered to return to your own country.

I ask it by your peaceful life in Nazareth where you met so many joys and sorrows.

I ask it by your great distress, when the adorable Child was lost to you and his Mother for three days. I ask it by your joy at finding him in the Temple, and by the comfort you found at Nazareth, while living in the company of the Child Jesus. I ask it by the wonderful submission he showed in his obedience to you.

I ask it by the perfect love and conformity you showed in accepting the divine order to depart from this life, and from the company of Jesus and Mary. I ask it by the joy which filled your soul, when the Redeemer of the world, triumphant over death and hell, entered into the possession of his kingdom and led you into it with special honors.

I ask it through Mary's glorious Assumption, and through that endless happiness you share with her in the presence of God.

O good father! I beg you, by all your sufferings, sorrows, and joys, to hear me and obtain for me what I ask. [Here name your petitions or think of them.]

Obtain for all those who have asked my prayers everything that is useful to them in the plan of God. Finally, my dear patron and father, be with me and all who are dear to me in our last *moments, that we may eternally sing the praises of JESUS, MARY and JOSEPH.*

A blameless life, St. Joseph, may we lead, by your patronage from danger freed.

This prayer may be said during any thirty days of the year. You may also say an Our Father, Hail Mary, and Glory Be each day for nine days or thirty days in place of the novena prayer. I happen to like the prayer above since it is in honor of the thirty years that St. Joseph spent with Jesus and Mary. I also pray other novena prayers to St. Joseph. I'm sure he doesn't mind what prayers you choose—just as long as you invoke his intercession.

— 34 —
ON PRAYER AND HOLINESS

St. Thérèse of Lisieux expressed what prayer meant to her. She said, "For me, prayer is a surge of the heart; it is a simple look turned toward heaven; it is a cry of recognition and of love, embracing both trial and joy." As mentioned earlier, St. John of the Cross teaches us: "Learn to abide with attention in loving waiting upon God in the state of quiet. Contemplation is nothing else but a secret, peaceful, and loving infusion of God, which, if admitted, will set the soul on fire with the Spirit of love." Let us mothers seek a little quiet here and there so that we may contemplate God's great love for mothers and families and hear his whispers to our souls. When it is difficult to find a quiet place or even peace in our own thoughts to formulate prayers, we can remain hopeful knowing that we are "infused" with Our Lord and can always remain in communication with him through our faithful hearts even when it appears difficult to do so.

Mother Teresa let us in on the secrets to sanctity. She said, "Sanctity is not a luxury for the few. It is a simple duty for you and me. I have to be a saint in my way and you in yours.

Thoughtfulness is the beginning of great sanctity. If you learn this art of being thoughtful, you will become more and more like Christ, for his heart was meek and he always thought of others."

St. Teresa of Avila offered her poignant words, "Patient endurance attains to all things. The one who possesses God is lacking in nothing; God alone is enough." Additionally, St. Teresa said, "Oh, virtue of obedience! It can do everything!" St. Philip Neri offered some very good prayer advice that we mothers can utilize daily. He said, "It is an old custom of the servants of God to have some little prayers ready and to be frequently darting them up to heaven during the day, lifting their minds to God out of the mire of this world." Mothers know all too well the need for offering up continual prayer and aspirations to Our Lord, asking for strength and grace. "Lord, I love you; please remain with me," or "Dear Jesus, please enlarge my heart to love more fervently throughout this day," and "Blessed Mother Mary, be a Mother to me as I mother my children this day" are all examples of prayers that we can offer up as we go about our business in the household.

Servant of God Archbishop Fulton J. Sheen was a remarkable preacher, and as far as I am concerned he is already a saint. Regarding our call to holiness and the circumstances that we find ourselves in, he said, "There are many who excuse themselves, saying that if they were in other circumstances they would be much more patient. This is a grave mistake, for it assumes that virtue is a matter of geography, and not of moral effort. It makes little difference where we are; it all depends on what we are thinking about." These are great words for mothers to take to heart. Our dear Lord puts us precisely where he wants us to be to work out our salvation and to help pave the path for our children and our husband. Let's pray that we can keep this in mind when someone in the family is cranky, disobedient, or unruly, or when our circumstances are not what we hope or what we had planned. God is in control at all times. We must pray that we can respond in love to whoever surrounds us and whatever situation we find ourselves in.

St. John Vianney spoke about the prayerful soul and God's tender love for us. He said, "The interior life is like a sea of love in which the soul is plunged and is, as it were, drowned in love. Just as a mother holds her child's face in her hands to cover it with kisses, so does God hold the devout man." I think this is such a beautiful depiction of a mother's love and Our Lord's love for us.

St. Francis of Assisi was straight to the point when he said, "Sanctify yourself and you will sanctify society." Time before Jesus in the Blessed Sacrament may seem scarce for a busy mom; however, we know that it is there with Jesus that we will receive many graces and blessings. Whenever it is pos-sible, a mother should ask her husband, a relative, or a good friend for assistance with her children so that she may steal away to be at the feet of Jesus. This will be a welcome change of pace for a hardworking mother, and will give her food for her soul so that she will be well nourished to continue her journey. I recommend bringing your children to Jesus in the Blessed Sacrament as well.

A number of saints have expressed their sentiments on Jesus in the Blessed Sacrament. I'll include a few for inspiration for us mothers. St. Anthony Mary Claret said, "When I am before the Blessed Sacrament I feel such a lively faith that I cannot describe it. Christ in the Eucharist is almost tangible to me. To kiss his wounds continually and embrace him. When it is time to leave I have to tear myself away from his sacred presence." I understand, St. Anthony Mary Claret. I feel the same way.

St. Thérèse of Lisieux spoke eloquently about Jesus coming to us in Holy Communion. She said, "Our Lord does not come down from heaven every day to be in a golden ciborium. He comes to find another heaven which is infinitely dearer to him—the heaven of our souls." Can I make a tabernacle in my soul for Our Lord? As we prepare our souls for Our Lord's presence, let us also receive him frequently in spiritual communions as often as we are able. When we cannot get to extra Masses or Holy Hours, we can always ask him to come into our souls and reside there in our loving hearts—our tabernacle for him. He will bless us and bless others through us. Let's not forget to ask him.

— 35 —

ST. MONICA AND
ST. AUGUSTINE

Pope Emeritus Benedict XVI spoke about St. Monica and St. Augustine as two saints who offer much hope to struggling families. Although they lived in the fourth century, Pope Benedict shared that "their testimonies can be of great consolation and help for many families also of our time." He explained that St. Monica's "mission of wife and mother" was exemplary. She helped "her husband, Patricius, to discover, little by little, the beauty of faith in Christ and the strength of evangelical love."

We also know that St. Monica's tears and prayers merited a transformation of heart for both her son, Augustine, and her husband. Even when St. Monica's situation must have seemed rather bleak and even impossible, she persevered in prayer— and we wives and mothers should too. Let's try to remember to have recourse to St. Monica for intercession for our families.

"As Augustine himself would say later," Pope Benedict continued, "his mother gave him birth twice; the second time required a long spiritual labor, made up of prayer and tears, but crowned in the end by the joy of seeing him not only embrace the faith and receive baptism, but also dedicate himself entirely to the service of Christ." He added: "How many difficulties there are also today in family relationships and how many mothers are anguished because their children choose mistaken ways!"

Benedict XVI added that St. Monica invites all mothers "not to be discouraged, but to persevere in their mission of wives and mothers, maintaining firm their confidence in God and clinging with perseverance to prayer." The pontiff also stated that St. Augustine is a "model of the way to God, supreme truth and good." Christian mothers can remain hopeful about their wayward children by looking to St. Augustine's intercession. Pope Benedict tells us that St. Augustine may "obtain for us also the gift of a sincere and profound encounter with Christ," especially "for all those young people who, thirsty for happiness, seek it in mistaken ways and get lost in dead ends."

In his talk to the crowds that gathered with him to pray the Angelus, the Bishop of Rome finished by entrusting to the Virgin Mary "Christian parents so that, like Monica, they will support their children on their way with their example and prayer, and young people so that, as Augustine, they will always tend to the fullness of truth and love, which is Christ." Pope Emeritus Benedict added that Christ "alone can satisfy the profound needs of the human heart."

I have given examples of saintly inspiration to give you a boost. I encourage you to research some saints on your own and learn more about our wonderful inspiring friends who are part of the Communion of Saints.

SOMETHING TO PONDER

Why should I pray to the saints?

RECIPE FOR SWEET AND SAVORY SAINTLY INSPIRATION

The saints were ordinary pilgrims like me, and they can help guide me on my own journey to heaven by interceding for me, asking for the graces I need. They transcend history and offer me timeless wisdom and inspiration.

IN THE SHADOW OF THE HOLY FAMILY

My life here in the heart of my home
Seems to be lived in the shadows,
At times hidden away from the bustle of the world,
Close to the hearth.
Help me, Lord, to strive to emulate a life of the
Holy Family's holiness,
To create another Nazareth in the cenacle of prayer of my home,
Allowing the light emanated from the Holy Family
To radiate throughout the shadows of my domestic church,
Brightening every corner!
Thank you, Lord, for the example of the Holy Family
and the saints
To help light our way to heaven!

— 36 —

EVANGELIZING THE HOUSEHOLD AND THE WORLD

*"You are the salt of the earth; but if salt
has lost its taste, how can its saltiness be
restored? It is no longer good for anything,
but is thrown out and trampled under foot.*
*"You are the light of the world. A city
built on a hill cannot be hid. No one after
lighting a lamp puts it under the bushel
basket, but on the lampstand, and it gives
light to all in the house. In the same way,
let your light shine before others, so that
they may see your good works and give
glory to your Father in heaven."*
—Matthew 5:13–16 (NRSVCE)

Blessed Jordan of Saxony has said, "So long as we are still in
this place of pilgrimage, so long as men's hearts are crooked
and prone to sin, lazy and feeble in virtue, we need to be
encouraged and roused, so that brother may be helped by

brother and the eagerness of heavenly love rekindle the flame in our spirit which our everyday carelessness and tepidity tend to extinguish." My former spiritual director and friend, Father John Hardon, SJ, spoke often about the great need for evangelization. He was always telling everyone who attended his retreats all that he knew about the call to evangelize. He would often say, "There's work to be done!" You couldn't escape that penetrating look from his eyes into yours when he made that statement—he meant *you!* And you knew it! Father Hardon wrote, "Catholics have to wake up to their grave responsibility in the modern world; they must be aroused from their sleep of lethargy in allowing the media to be mainly untapped for the extension of Christ's Kingdom in our day."

In our *Catechism* we also find words of direction regarding our responsibilities to evangelize as a Christian family in our world:

Christ chose to be born and grow up in holiness in the bosom of the holy family of Joseph and Mary. The Church is nothing other than "the family of God." From the beginning, the core of the Church was often constituted by those who had become believers "together with all [their] household." When they were converted, they desired that "their whole household" should also be saved. These families who became believers were islands of Christian life in an unbelieving world.

In our own time, in a world often alien and even hostile to faith, believing families are of primary importance as centers of living, radiant faith. For this reason, the Second Vatican Council, using an ancient expression, calls the family the *Ecclesia domestica*. It is in the bosom of the family that parents are "by word and example . . . the first heralds of the faith with regard to their children. They should encourage them in the vocation which is proper to each child, fostering with special care any religious vocations.

It is here that the father of the family, the mother, children, and all members of the family exercise the *priesthood of the baptized* in a privileged way "by the reception of the sacraments, prayer, and thanksgiving, the witness of a holy life, and self-denial and active charity." Thus the home is the first school of Christian life and "a school for human enrichment." Here one learns endurance and the joy of work, fraternal love, generous—even repeated forgiveness, and above all divine worship in prayer and the offering of one's own life. (CCC, 1655–58)

As mothers busy with many things in our households, how can we even pause to consider that we may have a role to play in evangelization in our world today? We are very preoccupied with the care of our families, after all. Perhaps we desire to be out there proclaiming the Good News, not hiding our light under a bushel basket, but here we are firmly planted within the hearts of our homes. How does evangelization apply to us? We must consider that the good Lord has chosen us to mother our brood and to do it wholeheartedly as well. We need to be content with evangelizing first within the walls of our homes where we begin the sanctification process for our families. Each day brings joys and challenges to live and breathe through. Each of our children is a unique human being requiring our attention in a variety of ways.

We have heard the phrase "to the ends of the earth!" Pope St. John Paul II, Pope Emeritus Benedict XVI, and Pope Francis have urged the faithful laity to live out their Christianity and take it to the streets—"to the ends of the earth"—and spread the gospel message to everyone there. We know that the first to do this were the followers of Jesus, the Apostles. Jesus even nicknamed Simon, Andrew, James, and John "fishers of men." They were very close to Jesus, so they were able to accurately bring his message to others. In the same way, we must get closer to Jesus through prayer and frequenting the sacraments of confession and Holy Communion so that we can bring Jesus's message to others— not our own versions of the Gospels, but the authentic Good News. We'll be able to do that once we surrender our lives totally over to Our Lord so that he can teach us and mold us throughout our daily lives. However, as mothers to our bustling and growing households, our "ends of the earth" will in actuality be to *the ends of the household* for a time. This is truly what Our Lord wants of us—to embrace our family's home life and be content in our mothering evangelization in the form of educating our children in the faith and in the atmosphere of prayer that we create within the hearts of our homes. Our example will make a deep impression on our children's hearts, not to ever be erased no matter what life throws at them in the future years.

As time rolls on and our children are growing, we find ourselves out and about in the community because of the various activities that they participate in. Our example as Christian mothers and our charity to others in many ways is a part of our evangelization in the world. Throughout the seasons of our lives, we will be given countless opportunities to evangelize.

Such opportunities can include working in a local soup kitchen together as a family. By the way, the Missionaries of Charity nuns appreciate occasional help feeding the poor in their soup kitchens. If you are fortunate enough to live within driving distance, I highly recommend that you look into the possibility. It's an amazing place to take your children to rub elbows with holiness! Once I had the wonderful experience of living with the sisters in Harlem, New York, while Father Hardon was giving a retreat for them. I was able to participate in their prayer and work and also help in the soup kitchen, something I will never forget. I actually slept in the women's shelter, and that was quite an experience in itself.

Sadly, we know all too well that there are many who have left the Church because of something they didn't like in a priest's homily or because of something they heard that a priest has done. The entire Catholic Church is judged or condemned because of a misunderstanding, disagreement, or even a real abuse. We probably all know at least one person who has left the Church because of something they didn't like about a priest or a parish. Whether they have good reason or not, this happens quite frequently.

Let's consider another occasion when someone may decide to leave the Church. Did you know that you are actually a reflection of the Catholic Church wherever you are and whatever you do? Yes, it's true. I know a very nice woman who left the Church because she heard women gossiping in the parish office. The woman became so turned off by the parish that she decided to leave the Church! While I don't understand why she would judge an entire Church because of a few women's bad behavior or lack of prudence, I do realize that this can happen. Let's keep this in mind as we are out and about in the community representing our Church. Our behavior and example is a form of evangelization. We certainly don't want to turn people away from the Church!

Another occasion to evangelize with your family is to visit a local nursing home or hospital with your children. Jesus calls us to visit the sick and lonely. You can set up times with the staff when you will visit the residents, hopefully choosing the ones who don't have family nearby and don't receive many (or any) visits. Taking the time to give a little love and cheer to someone who is just aching to be heard—even if it is the same story over and over again that they love to tell—will bring abundant blessings not only to the recipient, but to you and your family as well. It's truly an amazing experience when giving to the less fortunate because we seem to receive much more than we attempted to bring to them. They are "Jesus in the distressing disguise of the poorest of the poor," as St. Teresa of Calcutta always used to say.

The possibilities are endless to help light others' lamps out in the world. Perhaps your family can pray together to seek guidance regarding what your family apostolate should be. Allow the children to voice their suggestions and opinions and help alleviate their possible fear of visiting the lonely. You will be together as a family, and your prayerful and joyful presence will bring great peace and happiness to others. You will also be setting an essential foundation of evangelizing and serving for your family. By God's grace, hopefully your children will be willing to carry on their charitable service and their Works of Mercy to others throughout their lives.

37

IT TAKES ONE

At one time our Blessed Mother was an ordinary but faithful teenage Jewish girl, striving with all her heart to follow God and her Jewish tradition. We know the marvelous Gospel account of when the angel Gabriel appeared to Mary, announcing that she would be the Mother of God!

> In the sixth month the angel Gabriel was sent by God to a town in Galilee called Nazareth, to a virgin engaged to a man whose name was Joseph, of the house of David. The virgin's name was Mary. And he came to her and said, "Greetings, favored one! The Lord is with you." But she was much perplexed by his words and pondered what sort of greeting this might be. The angel said to her, "Do not be afraid, Mary, for you have found favor with God. And now, you will conceive in your womb and bear a son, and you will name him Jesus. He will be great, and will be called the Son of the Most High, and the Lord God will give to him the throne of his ancestor David. He will reign over the house of Jacob forever, and of his kingdom there will be no end." Mary said to the angel, "How can this be, since I am a virgin?" The angel said to her, "The Holy Spirit will come upon you, and the power of the Most High will overshadow

you; therefore the child to be born will be holy; he will
be called Son of God. And now, your relative Elizabeth in
her old age has also conceived a son; and this is the sixth
month for her who was said to be barren. For nothing will
be impossible with God." Then Mary said, "Here am I, the
servant of the Lord; let it be with me according to your word."
Then the angel departed from her. (Lk. 1:26–39, NRSVCE)

Yes, Mary was the mother of Jesus and was favored by
God, but she was just *one* woman and said her *one* "yes" wholeheartedly and courageously to follow God's holy will in her
life. Her simple yet tremendous "yes" indeed changed the
world for all eternity.

Let's consider St. Teresa of Calcutta, whom I was
privileged to know for almost ten years. She was thought to
be ordinary by her fellow nuns when she first entered the
convent. Yet it was within her ordinariness and humility that
she responded with her extraordinary "yes" to God to take
care of his poorest of the poor. This one simple woman who
was small in stature made a remarkable impact on the entire
world because she decided to follow God's holy will for her
own life, which, in the final analysis, affected thousands upon
thousands of people and more accurately affected the entire
world—forever! Because of Mother Teresa we came to see
that starvation is not simply a problem in the third-world
countries. We became more aware of the plight of those in
our modern Western world who are starving for love.

Now let's recall the account of a young boy who answered Jesus directly with his "yes." He was the boy who gave Jesus his loaves and fish when Jesus asked if he could have them to feed the hungry crowd.

And they went away in the boat to a deserted place by themselves. Now many saw them going and recognized them, and they hurried there on foot from all the towns and arrived ahead of them. As he went ashore, he saw a great crowd; and he had compassion for them, because they were like sheep without a shepherd; and he began to teach them many things. When it grew late, his disciples came to him and said, "This is a deserted place, and the hour is now very late; send them away so that they may go into the surrounding country and villages and buy something for themselves to eat." But he answered them, "You give them something to eat." They said to him, "Are we to go and buy two hundred denarii worth of bread, and give it to them to eat?" And he said to them, "How many loaves have you? Go and see." When they had found out, they said, "Five, and two fish." Then he ordered them to get all the people to sit down in groups on the green grass. So they sat down in groups of hundreds and of fifties. Taking the five loaves and the two fish, he looked up to heaven, and blessed and broke the loaves, and gave them to his disciples to set before the people; and he divided the two fish among them all. And all ate and were filled; and they took up twelve baskets full of broken pieces and of the fish. Those who had eaten the loaves numbered five thousand men. (Mk. 6:32–44, NRSVCE)

A boy was asked by Jesus for his meager five pieces of bread and two fish that would ultimately be used to feed thousands. Because of the generosity of this young man, this story made it to the Gospel pages in the Bible to be pondered and studied throughout history.

One "yes"—yours and mine—can move mountains, open our eyes, transform hearts, feed thousands, and change history according to God's grace and his holy will.

I have used these three examples so that you will not be afraid with your "yes" to God and so you will realize that one person can make a tremendous difference to our world when he or she is cooperating with God's holy will in their life.

Our Lord calls us to be salt and light to the world. In Matthew 5 we learn that if salt loses its taste, it goes bad and becomes useless, just trampled underfoot. We are also told that our lights aren't to be hidden under a bushel! We must go forward putting one foot in front of the other each day to walk in faith and be salt and light to the world within all our walks of life—throughout our busy days in our domestic churches where we help to work out the salvation for our families and out in our communities and in the world. Our Lord gives us an awesome task. It is up to us to wake up from our slumber and ask for the graces to become aware of our mission in this world. We can then answer God with our wholehearted "yes!" It has to be wholehearted! No wishy-washy or wimpy yeses are allowed here.

I will also leave you with the following passage from the Bible to ponder. We are told that Our Lord allows the wheat to grow with the weeds (Matt. 13:24–30). I believe in miracles. Let's be patient in all of our dealings with all those whom God in his divine providence has put in our midst. The weeds of today may become the wheat of tomorrow, by God's miraculous grace and our example. We are allowed to grow together. Our Lord is a God of umpteen chances. He gives us a lifetime of chances to turn to him. Let's let our lights shine and become that example of holiness to those who may be struggling or who have been deceived, and let's inspire them to the blessedness of our Christianity, by God's amazing grace! In so doing, the world will indeed be changed—one person and one family at a time—to become the brightest beacon of Christ's love ever! I am reminded of Father Hardon's encouragement and strong desire to get everyone motivated to do God's work. Again, he simply said, "There's work to be done!" I will add: It must start with us right now. Let's do it!

May God bless you and your beautiful family now and forever!

SOMETHING TO PONDER

As a mother who is busy with so many things, how can I even consider adding evangelization to my plate?

RECIPE FOR REACHING OUT

Evangelization can be woven into my day-to-day life. Through my mothering in my household and during my time spent out in my community and the world, I open myself to God's graces so that I can be a light to others.

SEASONS

There are many seasons in a mother's life.
When her baby is young,
She needs to be near him and with him,
Ever present, devoting herself to his constant care,
Happy to be his source of comfort and love.
As her child grows older,
Navigating life and finding his way,
A mother stands nearby, always ready to guide,
Ever loving and steady.
Her older growing child allows her a little freedom
To administer to the needs of her neighbor.
By her loving example,
Her child learns to open his heart to those around him,
Listening for the cries of the poor.
He, too, one day will give of himself,

Being another source of comfort and love.
Our Lord will be pleased.
And so will his mom!

Dear Lord Jesus, please, grant us your graces.
Queen of the most holy Rosary, pray for us!

ACKNOWLEDGMENTS

For all of the mothers in my life:
Thank you for mothering me!

To my mother, Alexandra Mary Uzwiak Cooper, in loving memory and gratitude for bringing me into this world against doctor's orders and for teaching me the necessity of prayer and how to give without ever counting the cost.

In loving memory and gratitude to my grandmother, Alexandra Theresa Karasiewicz Uzwiak, for her inexhaustible love, guidance, and inspiration.

To my godmother, Aunt Bertha Uzwiak Barosky, in gratitude for her loving prayers and guidance throughout my life.

In loving memory of St. Teresa of Calcutta, with my gratitude for her inspiration and her consistent encouragement to me to continue to write to help others, especially mothers, which has certainly given me much courage and motivation. Her faith in me, her prayers, and her love for me have left a permanent imprint on my heart.

To dear Mother Mary, our Blessed Mother, who has always watched over me during my lifetime, in gratitude for her motherly influence, love, and protection that has forever been my saving grace.

To All Others I Hold Dear

In loving memory of my father, Eugene Joseph Cooper, who along with my mother brought me into this world—my gratitude for his love and support, working hard to care for our large family.

To my brothers and sisters, Alice Jean, Gene, Gary, Barbara, Tim, Michael, and David, thank you for your love.

To my husband, David, my partner and best friend, thank you for believing in me and loving me. I love you.

My children are my greatest joy in life: Justin, Chaldea, Jessica, Joseph, and Mary-Catherine. My grandchildren, Shepherd James and Leo Arthur, bless me with unending joy. May God continue to bless all of you. I love you so much!

With grateful thanks and loving memory to my dear friend and spiritual guide, Father William C. Smith, for his cherished friendship, love, and blessed guidance.

With grateful thanks and loving memory to my friend, my spiritual guide, and my daughter's godfather, Father John A. Hardon, SJ, for his marvelous wisdom, continued prayers, and guidance from heaven!

With grateful thanks and loving memory to my dear friend and spiritual guide Father Andrew Apostoli, CFR, for his precious friendship and spiritual wisdom.

In loving memory of dear St. John Paul the Great, with my gratitude for his inexhaustible wisdom and blessings in the profound and selfless love of his shepherding, which I was able to benefit from throughout a good part of my lifetime.

I especially wish to thank the wonderful folks at Paraclete Press: Robert Edmonson and Jon Sweeney, as well as the excellent team who worked hard to get this book out to you!

Lastly, with heartfelt gratefulness, I want to thank my readers for their friendship and prayers for my journey. I hope they will feel assured of my continued prayers for all of them in their own personal journeys. I hope that they will also know that we are all in this together on the road that leads to Life! Let's continue to pray for one another! God love you!

Donna-Marie Cooper O'Boyle speaks to a mother's heart about the blessings, challenges, grace, and lessons learned throughout her spiritual journey during motherhood. She has received numerous awards for her work and is the best-selling, award-winning author of more than twenty-five books, including her memoir *The Kiss of Jesus: How Mother Teresa and the Saints Helped Me to Discover the Beauty of the Cross.* Donna-Marie grew up in a large, close-knit Catholic family, admiring God's majesty in the beauty of nature surrounding her as she sought out holiness and searched for a deeper meaning in life. Embracing family life, she became a wife and mother of five and is now a proud grandmother. She also served as a prioress and mistress of novices for the Third Order of St. Dominic branch that she helped to start; founded a branch of the Lay Missionaries of Charity (Mother Teresa's order); taught religious education for over thirty years; and is an Extraordinary Minister of the Eucharist at her parish.

In God's divine providence, Donna-Marie met Servant of God Father John Hardon, SJ, who became her friend and spiritual director. She also met St. Teresa of Calcutta and remained in contact with her for a decade through correspondence and visits. Donna-Marie is passionate about sharing with other mothers her inspiration and "heart-to-hearts" that she had with her beloved friend Mother Teresa, as well as her own personal experiences and insights to encourage mothers and help them to see the sublimity in their vocation of motherhood.

The Holy See through the Pontifical Council for the Laity invited Donna-Marie to Rome in February 2008 to participate in an International Congress, "Woman and Man: The 'Humanum' in Its Entirety," on the occasion of the twentieth anniversary of *Mulieris Dignitatem*, "On the Dignity and Vocation of Women."

Donna-Marie's work has been featured in several Catholic magazines and national newspapers, and on several websites and Internet columns. Some of her articles have been featured in *L'Osservatore Romano*, *Magnificat* magazine, the *National Catholic Register*, *Our Sunday Visitor Newsweekly*, and more. She has been profiled on many television shows, including *Fox News*, *EWTN News Nightly*, *Rome Reports*, *Vatican Insider*, *EWTN Bookmark*, *Women of Grace*, *Sunday Night Prime*, *EWTN Live*, *At Home with Jim and Joy*, *The Journey Home*, and *Faith & Culture* on EWTN. She is a regular guest on many national radio shows as well, and has hosted her own show.

Donna-Marie is the EWTN television host of three series: *Everyday Blessings for Catholic Moms*, *Catholic Mom's Cafe*, and *Feeding Your Family's Soul*. She leads pilgrimages to a variety of holy sites and shrines throughout the world and lectures on topics relating to Catholic and Christian women, faith, and families. She can be reached at her websites, www .donnacooperoboyle.com and www.feedingyourfamilyssoul .com, where she also maintains blogs.

NOTES

5   *Every human person owes his or her life to a mother:* Pope Francis, General audience, January 7, 2015.

6   *Mothers are the strongest antidote:* Pope Francis, General Audience, January 27, 2015 (https://w2.vatican.va/content/francesco/en/audiences/2015/documents/papa-francesco_20150107_udienza-generale.html).

7   *It is a disservice not only to children:* St. John Paul II, letter, May 26, 1995 (https://w2.vatican.va/content/john-paul-ii/en/letters/1995/documents/hf_jp-ii_let_19950526_mongella-pechino.html).

12   *We are all called to be saints:* Pope Francis, General Audience, November 19, 2014, as described by Vatican Radio (http://en.radiovaticana.va/news/2014/11/19/pope_at_audience_the_universal_call_to_holiness/1111603).

19   *Sanctification is being made holy:* John Hardon, *Catholic Dictionary: An Abridged and Updated Edition of Modern Catholic Dictionary* (New York: Image, 2013), 456.

21   *To a great extent the level of any civilization:* Fulton Sheen, *Life Is Worth Living* (San Francisco: Ignatius, 1953).

22   *It is for us to become holy here and now:* St. Maximilian Kolbe, *Will to Love: Reflections for Daily Living* (Libertyville, IL: Marytown, 2013).

30   *Heroic virtue is the performance:* Hardon, *Catholic Dictionary.*

45   *From their conception:* Pope Emeritus Benedict XVI, address to participants, myself included, at the International Congress in Rome, "Woman and Man: The 'Humanum' in Its Entirety," February 2008 (https://zenit.org/articles/papal-address-to-participants-in-congress-on-women/).

47n1   *May mothers, young women, and girls:* Javier Abad, *Marriage, A Path to Sanctity* (San Antonio Village, Makati, Philippines: Sinag-tala, 2002), 131.

47n2   *God entrusts to women and to men:* Pope Emeritus Benedict XVI, address to participants at the International Congress "Woman and Man."

51   *The only essential is that one finds:* Edith Stein, *Self-Portrait in Letters, 1916-1942,* in *The Collected Works of Edith Stein,* vol. 5 (Washington, DC: ICS Publications, 1999).

53   *Every home is called to become a 'domestic Church':* Pope Emeritus Benedict XVI, General Audience, July 4, 2007 (http:// w2.vatican.va/content/benedict-xvi/en/audiences/2007/ documents/hf_ben-xvi_aud_20070704.html).

74   *To decorate the houses with religious pictures:* St. John Vianney in Ronda De Sola Chervin, *Quotable Saints* (Oak Lawn, IL: CMJ Marian Publishers, 2003), 79.

80   *the day or eve before a more or less prominent feast:* Hardon, *Catholic Dictionary.*

83   *"dead bodies float downstream":* Fulton Sheen in Henry Dietrick, compiler, *Through the Year with Fulton Sheen* (San Francisco: Ignatius, 2003), 28.

86   *Love to pray:* Roswitha Kornprobst, trans., School Sisters of Notre Dame, *Praying with Mother Teresa* (Mahwah NJ: Paulist, 2011), vii.

96   *Woman's soul is fashioned:* St. Teresa Benedicta of the Cross (Edith Stein), "Fundamental Principles of Women's Education," in Johnette Benkovic, *Graceful Living: Meditations to Help You Grow Closer to God Day by Day* (Irondale, AL: EWTN, 2016), 417.

109   *For a stalk to grow:* Pope St. John Paul II, General Audience, July 26, 2000.

112n1 *Frequent and exclusive breast-feeding delays ovulation and fertility:* NFP expert Sheila Kipley writes about this quite a bit in her books

The Seven Standards of Ecological Breastfeeding and *Breastfeeding and Catholic Motherhood*: The La Leche League International is a wonderful resource and support for breast-feeding moms. Their help line is (877) 452-5324; their website is www.llli.org.

112n2 *Saint Francis de Sales, that great saint*: Jull Haak Adels, *The Wisdom of the Saints: An Anthology* (New York, Oxford University Press, 1989), 60.

117 *Contemplation is nothing*: St. John of the Cross, *The Collected Works of St. John of the Cross: The Dark Night of the Soul*, Vol. II, "Spiritual Canticle of the Soul and the Bridegroom Christ, the Living Flame of Love," trans. David Lewis (New York, Cosimo Classics, 2007), 39.

137 *Humanity's future depends*: John Paul II, *Lessons for Living*, ed. Joseph Durepos (Chicago, Loyola, 2004), #6.

140 *The disagreeable experience of soul*: Hardon, *Catholic Dictionary*.

145n1 *In this sad world, there is a joy*: Charles de Foucauld, *Spiritual Autobiography of Charles de Foucauld*, ed. Jean François Six (New York: P. J. Kenedy, 1964), 19.

145n2 *The soul of one who loves God*: Donna-Marie Cooper O'Boyle, *A Catholic Woman's Book of Prayers* (Brewster, MA: Paraclete Press, 2017).

146 *If God causes you to suffer much*: St. Ignatius Loyola, in James J. McGovern, *The Manual of the Holy Catholic Church* (Chicago: Catholic Art and Publication Office, 1906), 264.

151 *I know, my God*: St. Thérèse from "An offering of myself as a holocaust victim to the merciful love of God," Testimony of Mother Agnes of Jesus (Prioress of the Lisieux Carmel), in *St. Therese of Lisieux by Those Who Knew Her (Testimonies from the Process of Beatification)*, trans. and ed. Christopher O'Mahony (Dublin, Ireland: Veritas, 1989), reprinted in http://www.parishbulletins .com/bulletins/218/April%2030%202017.pdf

154   *Let us all become a true and fruitful branch:* Donna-Marie Cooper
      O'Boyle, *Bringing Lent Home with Mother Teresa* (Notre Dame, IN:
      Ave Maria Press, 2012), "Fourth Sunday of Lent."

155n1 *Here on earth:* Poem by St. Thérèse of Lisieux.

155n2 *Without the burden of afflictions:* St. Rose of Lima in Carol Kelly-
       Gangi, *365 Days with the Saints: A Year of Wisdom from the Saints*
       (New York: Wellfleet Press, 2015), 168.

155n3 *Before I entered, when I woke up in the morning:* Brother Francis Mary,
       FFI, ed., *St. Thérèse: Doctor of the Little Way* (San Francisco: Ignatius,
       1998), 50.

156   *Melancholy is the poison of devotion:* St. Clare of Assisi in Chervin,
      Quotable Saints, 174.

157n1 *Let the brothers ever avoid appearing gloomy:* St. Francis of Assisi in
       Chervin, *Quotable Saints*, 174.

157n2 *Our labor here is brief:* St. Clare of Assisi in Chervin, *Quotable Saints*, 41.

157n3 *The sufferings God inflicts on contemplatives:* St. Teresa of Avila in
       Chervin, *Quotable Saints*, 175.

166n1 *For me, prayer is a surge of the heart:* St. Thérèse of Lisieux in *Catechism
       of the Catholic Church: Part Four: Christian Prayer: Section One:
       Prayer in the Christian Life* #2558 (St. Therese of Lisieux,
       Manuscrits autobiographiques, C 25r.).

166n2 *Learn to abide with attention:* St. John of the Cross in Chervin,
       Quotable Saints, 42.

166n3 *Sanctity is not a luxury for the few:* Mother Teresa in Jayla Chaliha
       and Edward Le Joly, compilers, *The Joy in Loving: A Guide to Daily
       Living* (New York: Penguin, 1996), June 27 reflection.

167n1 *Patient endurance attains to all things:* paraphrase of St. Teresa of
       Avila's Prayer at https://www.ewtn.com/devotionals/prayers
       /StTeresaofAvila.htm

167n2 *Oh, virtue of obedience!:* St. Teresa of Avila, *Saint Teresa of Avila
       Collection* [6 Books] By Saint Teresa of Avila, Aeterna Press,
       Chapter XVIII, The Fourth State of Prayer, # 10

167n3 *It is an old custom of the servants of God:* St. Philip Neri in Chervin, *Quotable Saints*, 42.

167n4 *There are many who excuse themselves:* Fulton J. Sheen, *Walk With God* (Staten Island, NY: Alba house, 2008), 60.

168 *The interior life is like a sea:* St. John Vianney in Bert Ghezzi, *The Voices of the Saints: A Year of Readings* (New York: Image Doubleday, 2002), 398.

169n1 *When I am before the Blessed Sacrament:* St. Anthony Mary Claret, *The Autobiography of St. Anthony Mary Claret,* (Compton, CA: Claretian Major Seminary, 1945), Chapter 6 pg. ?.

169n2 *Our Lord does not come down:* St. Thérèse of Lisieux in Francis W. Johnston, sel. and arr., *The Voice of the Saints: Counsels from the Saints to Bring Comfort and Guidance in Daily Living,* (London, UK: Burn and Oats, 1965), [pages unnumbered].

170 *Pope Emeritus Benedict XVI spoke about St. Monica and St. Augustine:* Pope Benedict XVI, Sunday Angelus address, August 27, 2006.

173 *So long as we are still in this place:* Adels, *The Wisdom of the Saints*, 105.

174 *Catholics have to wake up:* John Hardon, (www.therealpresence.org/archives/Media/Media_003.htm).

177 *Once I had the wonderful experience of living with the sisters:* This is recounted in my books about St. Teresa of Calcutta, *Mother Teresa and Me: Ten Years of Friendship* and *The Kiss of Jesus: How Mother Teresa and the Saints Helped Me to Discover the Beauty of the Cross.*

The MOUNT TABOR BOOKS series focuses on the arts and literature as well as liturgical worship and spirituality; it was created in conjunction with the Mount Tabor Ecumenical Centre for Art and Spirituality in Barga, Italy.

Music

The PARACLETE RECORDINGS label represents the internationally acclaimed choir *Gloriæ Dei Cantores*, the *Gloriæ Dei Cantores Schola*, and the other instrumental artists of the *Arts Empowering Life Foundation*.

Paraclete Press is the exclusive North American distributor for the Gregorian chant recordings from St. Peter's Abbey in Solesmes, France. Paraclete also carries all of the Solesmes chant publications for Mass and the Divine Office, as well as their academic research publications.

In addition, PARACLETE PRESS SHEET MUSIC publishes the work of today's finest composers of sacred choral music, annually reviewing over 1,000 works and releasing between 40 and 60 works for both choir and organ.

Video

Our DVDs offer spiritual help, healing, and biblical guidance for a broad range of life issues including grief and loss, marriage, forgiveness, facing death, understanding suicide, bullying, addictions, Alzheimer's, and Christian formation.

Learn more about us at our website:
www.paracletepress.com
or phone us toll-free at 1.800.451.5006

SCAN
TO
READ
MORE